50-103

Columbia University

Contributions to Education

Teachers College Series

No. 740

AMS PRESS
NEW YORK

SELECTION OF TEACHERS
IN
LARGE CITY SCHOOL SYSTEMS

By John Coulbourn   146578

SUBMITTED IN PARTIAL FULFILLMENT OF THE REQUIREMENTS FOR
THE DEGREE OF DOCTOR OF PHILOSOPHY IN THE FACULTY
OF PHILOSOPHY, COLUMBIA UNIVERSITY

Published with the Approval of
Professor Willard S. Elsbree, Sponsor

BUREAU OF PUBLICATIONS
TEACHERS COLLEGE, COLUMBIA UNIVERSITY
NEW YORK
1938

Library of Congress Cataloging in Publication Data

Coulbourn, John, 1888-
  Selection of teachers in large city school systems.

  Reprint of the 1938 ed., issued in series: Teachers
College, Columbia University. Contributions to edu-
cation, no. 740.
  Originally presented as the author's thesis, Columbia.
  Bibliography: p.
  1. Teachers--United States--Selection and appointment.
I. Title. II. Series: Columbia University. Teachers
College. Contributions to education, no. 740.
LB2835.C6 1972   658.31'12   72-176673
ISBN 0-404-55740-6

Reprinted by Special Arrangement with Teachers
College Press, New York, New York

From the edition of 1938, New York
First AMS edition published in 1972
Manufactured in the United States

AMS PRESS, INC.
NEW YORK, N. Y.   10003

ACKNOWLEDGMENTS

THE author is greatly indebted to the many school executives, supervisory officers, and teachers who contributed to this study. Without their cooperation the study would have been impossible.

To the members of his dissertation committee at Teachers College, Columbia University, Professors Willard S. Elsbree, Edward S. Evenden, and Arthur T. Jersild, he wishes to express his gratitude and appreciation for their suggestions and constructive criticisms. He is particularly indebted to Professor Elsbree, who indicated the significance of the study and served as its sponsor.

To his wife, Mary Hamilton Coulbourn, for her constant inspiration and encouragement, he wishes to acknowledge his indebtedness and to express his deepest appreciation.

J. C.

CONTENTS

vii

PART III. GENERAL SUMMARY AND RECOMMENDATIONS

PART IV. BIBLIOGRAPHY

PART I

Development of Problem, the Criteria, and the Organization

CHAPTER I

THE DEVELOPMENT OF THE PROBLEM

INTRODUCTION

PROBABLY the most important duty confronting the administration of the public schools is that of securing the most competent teachers. Upon this one thing more than any other depends the success or failure in the education and training of the American youth. As Cubberley[1] stated years ago, schools exist solely for the education of children, and not to provide employment for teachers. Moreover, it is contended by Graves[2] that appointment to a teaching position in the public school should be considered a privilege, not a right; it is a privilege granted the applicant who plans to make teaching a life work, not a stepping-stone to a more lucrative position in business, industry, or some other profession.

In our public schools only the best education should be provided, but this can be done only when the best teachers have been selected and most advantageously assigned. This important function of teacher selection becomes more evident when the administrator realizes that it is the teacher who will make or not make the proper and the most efficient use of the school building, grounds, and equipment; that it is the teacher who, in the last analysis, will interpret effectively or otherwise the curricula in terms of the needs of the pupils; and that it is the teacher who becomes the chief factor in building up an efficient system of schools. As Engelhardt has so aptly put it, "The most satisfactory means of raising administrative and teaching effectiveness is to improve the personnel. This can be done by training those who are employed while in service and by adopting a more discriminating plan for selecting and appointing persons to fill vacancies and new positions." [3]

[1] Cubberley, Ellwood P., *The Portland Survey*, p. 63. 1915.
[2] Graves, Frank P., *Report of a Survey of the Public Schools of New Rochelle, New York*, p. 120. 1936.
[3] Engelhardt, Fred, *Public School Organization and Administration*, p. 165. 1931.

According to Draper, "People are coming to realize that no school can be good, can do what it ought for its children or for the common good, can prepare for the rivalries of life, satisfy civic pride, or connect with the schools to which it is tributary, unless it is constantly on the lookout for the best teachers." [4] Thus the problem of teacher selection becomes something more than a mere administrative one. It is a matter of vital significance to every citizen in the school community—a significance which is so often overlooked or treated lightly. This view is further strengthened by Elsbree, who states: "The fate of society rests in the teachers' hands to a far greater extent than the layman realizes. Upon their skill, their knowledge, and their personal influence depends not only the immediate welfare of the pupils under them, but the shaping of tomorrow's citizenry." [5] Certain it is that the interests of both the pupils and the public in the welfare of the school are too great to be imperiled by neglect, ignorance, or non-professional procedures in the selection of teachers. A school administrator, charged with the interests both of the pupils and of the public, is rendering one of the most expert services he can render his community when he plans for the proper selection of his teachers. It behooves him, therefore, with the aid of his board of education to establish those procedures or methods of selection which will insure the best qualified teacher for each position to be filled. On his ability to secure and hold such qualified teachers, more than anything else, will depend the success of his school system. On the other hand, failure or neglect to carry out effectively this important administrative function breaks down professional standards, results in poor classroom teaching, retards the work of supervision, adds to the cost of education, and causes much waste in educational results. Lewis believes that "the greatest source of waste in education results from faulty adjustments between the teacher and her work, largely due to wrong selection and placement." [6]

Thus it can be said that there is no more important administrative responsibility than the proper selection of teachers. Any improved, systematic method or procedure for the selection of teachers will have

---

[4] Draper, A. S., *American Education*, p. 355. 1909.
[5] Elsbree, Willard S., *Teachers' Salaries*, p. 2. 1931.
[6] Lewis, Ervin E., *Personnel Problems of the Teaching Staff*, p. 140. 1925.

far-reaching results. It will provide better training for the children entrusted to the teachers in our schools and it will go far to eliminate much of the time and money wasted on the "trials and failures" as well as on poor teaching. It will tend further to establish teaching as a real profession.

PURPOSES OF THE STUDY

The problem of teacher selection takes on added importance and responsibility in the larger city school systems where the administrators' duties are so complex and deal with such large numbers of individuals. At the same time there are present the cross currents of political influence, social "pull," and local favoritism; the injection of personalities into professional matters; and the constant attempts of local organizations to promote their interests—all of which make an effective merit system of teacher selection more imperative. Moreover, the complex organization of a large city system, with its many different types and classifications of teaching positions (primary, intermediate, junior high, senior high, secondary, special, prevocational, commercial, vocational, and many others), makes it mandatory that teachers be chosen for specific positions which demand special training.

These general aspects of large city school systems require definite administrative procedures for selecting teachers. It is true that certain procedures are ignored or deemed unnecessary in some systems, while these same procedures are considered most worth while or are overemphasized in others. Some procedures are found to be in general use but differing widely in character, scope, and importance. Although more or less definite standards of practice relating to some of the separate administrative aspects of teacher selection have been developed through research studies, there is a real need for a comprehensive survey of the practices in the field of teacher selection brought up to date, covering each important step in the entire administrative procedure, and presented as a complete program. It is the purpose of this study, then, to survey the practices now current, evaluate them in the light of basic criteria, and establish more effective standards for procedures and methods in the field of teacher selection.

OBJECTIVES OF THE STUDY

Because of this need for more adequate information and professional guidance in the field of teacher selection, this study proposes:

A. To set up the criteria or basic principles which should govern administrative procedures in teacher selection.

B. To survey the present practices followed in large city school systems in the selection of teachers.

C. To evaluate such practices in the light of the criteria or basic principles set up.

D. On the basis of such descriptive and critical evaluation, to recommend procedures in teacher selection which will more adequately and efficiently serve the best interests of public education.

SCOPE OF THE PROBLEM

Since this study lies chiefly in the field of school administration, it deals primarily with the procedures and methods which school authorities follow in selecting teachers. In other words, it concerns itself with the administrative program which is set up for the effective discharge of this important administrative function and considers the following aspects of the problem:

A. Responsibility for teacher selection.

B. Organization of personnel departments, boards of examiners, and groups in charge of teacher selection.

C. Sources of supply of teachers.

D. Methods of securing information about applicants.

E. Methods of checking and evaluating information about applicants.

F. Oral and written examinations.

G. Physical examinations.

H. Interviews.

I. Demonstration of teaching ability.

J. Qualifications and requirements.

K. Eligible or merit lists.

L. Probationary service.

M. Recruitment for teacher training.

N. Cooperation of teacher-training institutions.

TABLE I

THE THIRTY-SEVEN LARGEST CITIES AND THEIR POPULATIONS

(United States Census, 1930)

City	Population
Akron, Ohio	255,040
Atlanta, Georgia	270,366
Baltimore, Maryland	804,874
Birmingham, Alabama	259,678
Boston, Massachusetts	781,188
Buffalo, New York	573,076
Chicago, Illinois	3,376,438
Cincinnati, Ohio	451,160
Cleveland, Ohio	900,429
Columbus, Ohio	290,564
Dallas, Texas	260,475
Denver, Colorado	287,861
Detroit, Michigan	1,568,662
Houston, Texas	292,352
Indianapolis, Indiana	364,161
Jersey City, New Jersey	316,715
Kansas City, Missouri	399,746
Los Angeles, California	1,238,048
Louisville, Kentucky	307,745
Memphis, Tennessee	253,143
Milwaukee, Wisconsin	578,249
Minneapolis, Minnesota	464,356
Newark, New Jersey	442,337
New Orleans, Louisiana	458,762
New York, New York	6,930,446
Oakland, California	284,063
Philadelphia, Pennsylvania	1,950,961
Pittsburgh, Pennsylvania	669,817
Portland, Oregon	301,815
Providence, Rhode Island	252,981
Rochester, New York	328,132
St. Louis, Missouri	821,960
St. Paul, Minnesota	271,606
San Francisco, California	634,394
Seattle, Washington	365,583
Toledo, Ohio	290,718
Washington, D.C.	486,869
Total Population	28,784,770

While the question of teacher selection is to be found in every school administrative unit, whether large or small, it seemed desirable to limit the study to a consideration of the problem in the largest cities. The time and cost involved in the study and the fact that every variety of practice was to be found in these cities justified their selection. Therefore, this study has been limited to the selection of teachers in the public school systems of those cities with populations of 250,000 or more, according to the United States Census of 1930. Table I lists these cities with their populations. These cities, thirty-seven in number, represent a total population of 28,784,770, or slightly more than 23 per cent of the total population of the Continental United States. They also represent nearly 42 per cent of the total population of the urban territory which includes all villages, towns, and cities with more than 2,500 inhabitants.

Table II gives the number of supervisors, principals, and teachers employed in the public schools of these thirty-seven cities for the years 1932 and 1934, as reported by the individual systems to the United States Department of the Interior, Office of Education. The number employed in 1932 was 144,779, including 6,594 principals and supervisors. Depression "economies" and reorganizations caused a slight drop in these totals for 1934, when the number of teachers employed was 141,464, including 6,411 principals and supervisors. These totals represent more than 16 per cent of the total number of teachers employed in all the public elementary and secondary schools in Continental United States. Moreover, they represent slightly more than 23 per cent of all public elementary and secondary school teachers in the twenty-three states and the District of Columbia where the thirty-seven largest cities are located.

SOURCES OF DATA

The data for the study have been collected principally from five sources:

1. Literature in the field of school administration and teacher selection.

2. All available printed and mimeographed materials from the thirty-seven cities studied. These materials included rules and regulations and administrative codes; records and reports of those di-

TABLE II

NUMBER OF SUPERVISORS AND PRINCIPALS AND TEACHERS EMPLOYED IN THE THIRTY–SEVEN LARGEST CITIES

(*Biennial Reports for 1932 and 1934, United States Office of Education*)

City	1932		1934	
	Supervisors and Principals	Teachers	Supervisors and Principals	Teachers
Akron, Ohio................	52	1,449	40	1,382
Atlanta, Georgia............	70	1,161	72	1,294
Baltimore, Maryland.........	222	3,527	169	3,402
Birmingham, Alabama.......	69	1,383	66	1,306
Boston, Massachusetts.......	170	3,990	156	4,193
Buffalo, New York...........	113	3,342	113	3,267
Chicago, Illinois.............	394	13,508	236	12,267
Cincinnati, Ohio.............	106	2,030	99	1,951
Cleveland, Ohio.............	270	4,437	235	4,122
Columbus, Ohio.............	81	1,405	70	1,260
Dallas, Texas...............	53	1,367	51	1,374
Denver, Colorado............	77	1,410	68	1,396
Detroit, Michigan...........	264	6,937	276	6,709
Houston, Texas..............	95	1,683	94	1,626
Indianapolis, Indiana........	131	1,866	123	1,753
Jersey City, New Jersey......	71	1,553	71	1,562
Kansas City, Missouri........	152	1,980	210	1,866
Los Angeles, California......	525	9,811	518	10,476
Louisville, Kentucky.........	87	1,359	82	1,363
Memphis, Tennessee.........	14	1,199	61	1,065
Milwaukee, Wisconsin........	133	2,572	130	2,484
Minneapolis, Minnesota......	137	2,628	119	2,546
Newark, New Jersey.........	87	2,472	66	2,408
New Orleans, Louisiana......	103	1,835	102	1,726
New York, New York........	1,720	32,643	1,628	32,093
Oakland, California..........	102	1,643	85	1,557
Philadelphia, Pennsylvania....	370	8,073	343	7,858
Pittsburgh, Pennsylvania.....	202	3,262	179	3,208
Portland, Oregon............	71	1,595	67	1,589
Providence, Rhode Island.....	75	1,541	77	1,468
Rochester, New York........	89	2,009	82	1,939
St. Louis, Missouri...........	179	2,728	167	2,839
St. Paul, Minnesota..........	77	1,316	69	1,359
San Francisco, California.....	149	2,403	138	2,509
Seattle, Washington..........	103	1,902	101	1,822
Toledo, Ohio................	68	1,445	64	1,338
Washington, D.C.............	143	2,821	144	2,876
Total................	6,594	138,185	6,411	135,053

rectly responsible for the selection of teachers; and copies of various blanks, forms, qualification requirements, instructions and information circulars, examination papers, rating plans, merit lists, and practice teaching records. They were obtained from the superintendent of schools personally, through his office, or from the administrative officer in charge of teacher selection.

3. Correspondence with the executives and supervisory officers in the thirty-seven cities who were directly responsible for the selection of teachers.

4. Personal interviews with such officers in ten of the cities which were visited.

5. Personal interviews with successful and unsuccessful candidates for teaching positions in seven of these cities.

TREATMENT OF THE DATA

The attempt throughout the study is to present the information regarding teacher selection procedures as practiced in these larger cities, to make an analysis of each step involved in these procedures, and to evaluate them in the light of certain criteria or basic principles which are held to govern the administration of teacher selection. Because of the scope of the study, involving thirty-seven cities representing all sections of the United States and including twenty-three states and the District of Columbia, financial and other limitations have somewhat restricted a more comprehensive description of some of the practices presented. The implications and conclusions resulting from the analysis and evaluation will at least point the way to better or more carefully planned procedures which will adequately serve the best interests of public education. As Henry Suzzallo has written, the way to better educational procedures is to be found "in thoughtful comparison, in appraisal of our richly diverse educational practices, and in selection and diffusion of the best accomplishment." [7]

[7] Suzzallo, Henry, "Schools of a People." *Twenty-Sixth Annual Report of the President and of the Treasurer of the Carnegie Foundation for the Advancement of Teaching*, p. 23. 1931.

CHAPTER II

CRITERIA FOR EVALUATING ADMINISTRATIVE PRACTICES AND ESTABLISHING STANDARDS OF TEACHER SELECTION

THE criteria which have been set up as bases for comparison and evaluation in this study are the result of a comprehensive study of available educational literature and a survey of prevailing practices and to some extent the trend of practice during recent years affecting the selection of teachers. Documentary validation of the criteria comes from two sources: competent authorities in general school administration and intensive research studies in special fields of teacher selection and school personnel.

The earliest important study of the problem of teacher selection in cities was made by Ballou in 1915.[1] This study was followed in 1928 by a survey of personnel practices in city school systems under the direction of the National Education Association.[2] These contributions dealt primarily with the responsibility of the superintendent for the selection of teachers and with the eligibility of candidates in terms of age, training requirements, teaching experience, health, and moral character. A more comprehensive survey, made in 1931 by the National Education Association, gave the most recent and representative data on some of the administrative practices in the selection and appointment of teachers.[3]

Besides these general surveys, rather extensive research studies made from time to time have dealt with separate procedures or factors in the problem of teacher selection. While these studies have not always considered practices and conditions in the larger city school systems, their findings have in many cases been accepted in whole or

---

[1] Ballou, Frank W., *Appointment of Teachers in Cities.* 1915.
[2] National Education Association, "Practices Affecting Teacher Personnel." *Research Bulletin,* Vol. VI, No. 4: 205–256, September, 1928.
[3] National Education Association, "Administrative Practices Affecting Classroom Teachers," Part I: The Selection and Appointment of Teachers. *Research Bulletin,* Vol. X, No. 1, January, 1932.

in part as authoritative and adaptable. Regarding some practices in the field of teacher selection, however, very little has been written. This lack of authoritative evidence and the difficulty found in measuring the influence of various practices upon the effectiveness of instruction make it impossible to have a formal statement on every criterion definitely affecting the subject.

However, every criterion proposed is substantiated by current practices and trends as revealed by the study. A comprehensive presentation of such practices is of great service since it makes possible a comparison of practices with general trends and establishes a practical basis for recommendations.

CRITERIA

The fundamental principles and standards of school administration which should govern teacher selection are based on the following criteria which are validated with accompanying documentary evidence taken from the writings of recognized authorities in school administration:

Criterion I

The ultimate responsibility for the selection of teachers rests with the superintendent of schools.

It is generally recognized among school administrators that the responsibility for the selection of teachers rests with the superintendent of schools and his assistants.[4]

It has long been recognized as a fundamental principle of administration that the superintendent of schools should be responsible for the recommendation for appointment of individuals to all professional offices as well as to other positions in the school system.[5]

To place the work of teacher selection on such a level is not easy, nor can it be done in a day. First, it requires the education of the whole community on this matter. The rank and file of the citizenry must come to recognize that the schools are maintained solely for the benefit of children, not as a means of providing employment to any group. Second, it calls for a school board which prides itself upon its ability to recognize the proper division of functions between itself and the superintend-

[4] "Administrative Practices Affecting Classroom Teachers," *op. cit.*, p. 23.
[5] Engelhardt, Fred, *Public School Organization and Administration*, p. 181. 1931.

ent and his staff as it concerns this important duty. The board, advised by the superintendent, will concentrate its energy upon the formulation of the principles and policies to govern the selection of teachers. To the superintendent, it will delegate all the work of putting these principles and policies into effective operation, and will hold him responsible for results.[6]

The selection of teachers is a function of the superintendent and is certainly the practice in most of our large cities.[7]

Criterion II

The selection of teachers should be based upon merit.

The schools exist, in no sense, to afford places for teachers. No one is entitled by right to a teacher's position, except on the one basis of being the best prepared and the most professionally in earnest teacher available.[8]

Qualifications should be the sole determining factor in appointment and promotion.[9]

State and national campaigns of education should be conducted to encourage school board members to select new teachers upon the basis of scholarship, special professional preparation, experience, and merit, rather than upon such bases as local residence, willingness to accept lower salaries, and similar factors.[10]

Many non-educational pressures revolve around the selection, placement, and management of the teaching staff. All decisions upon questions arising out of such pressure should be made on a rigorously professional basis.[11]

He [the superintendent] should himself hold, and constantly impress upon the board that the only relevant consideration in selecting teachers is the efficiency of the candidate.[12]

In the large city school systems the plan of selecting teachers from a merit list has been found the most practicable and successful.[13]

[6] Strayer, George D., *Report of the Survey of the Schools of Fort Worth, Texas*, p. 304. 1931.
[7] Reeder, Ward G., *The Fundamentals of Public School Administration*, p. 57. 1930.
[8] Cubberley, Ellwood P., *The Portland Survey*, p. 308. 1915.
[9] National Education Association, *Code of Ethics*, Article II, Section 5. 1926.
[10] National Survey of the Education of Teachers, Vol. II: *Teacher Personnel in the United States*, p. 104. 1935.
[11] Strayer, George D., *Report of the Survey of the Schools of Chicago, Illinois*, Vol. I, p. 248. 1932.
[12] Graves, Frank P., *The Administration of American Education*, p. 193. 1932.
[13] Engelhardt, Fred, *op. cit.*, p. 181.

Criterion III

An efficient program of teacher selection demands some type of organization responsible for the activities having to do with personnel management.

The function of securing and maintaining the best possible teaching force, and providing the best conditions for their work, is second to no administrative consideration in the school system. Moreover, in a large city it is so complex in its activities and deals with such large groups of persons and masses of information, that it becomes the leading administrative sub-division. These reasons alone are sufficient to indicate the urgency of the need for a department of personnel.[14]

These functions of the superintendent relating to the selection of teachers are so vital and exacting that it would be well in a school system of any size to organize a teachers' bureau or personnel office. . . . There is still urgent need of personnel officers attached to the superintendent's staff who shall find more scientific methods of keeping incompetents out of various positions and of placing all teachers where they can serve with most satisfaction and profit.[15]

More recently, departments of personnel have been organized in many of the large cities. All the problems which have to do with selection, retention, salaries, promotion, and training are referred to this department. . . . The development of personnel departments in school systems makes it possible for the superintendent to centralize the activities associated with personnel management.[16]

Experience and research, however, have revealed certain principles and practices which will guarantee the children of a city the services of a well qualified teaching staff. Such a staff is purchasable. The price is a carefully planned, skillfully executed program of personnel administration.[17]

Criterion IV

The superintendent, or his authorized agents, should actively seek desirable candidates for the teaching staff.

A well-established principle is that the superintendent or his representative should actively seek desirable candidates.[18]

[14] *Report of the Survey of the Schools of Chicago, Illinois,* Vol. I, p. 248.
[15] Graves, Frank P., *op. cit.,* pp. 201–202.
[16] Engelhardt, Fred, *op. cit.,* pp. 181–182, 217.
[17] *Report of the Survey of the Schools of Fort Worth, Texas,* p. 294.
[18] "Administrative Practices Affecting Classroom Teachers," *op. cit.,* p. 23.

The importance of seeking the best incumbents wherever they may be found, inside the system or out, cannot be too strongly emphasized.[19]

A school system should not depend upon the chance receipt of applications as a means of locating good teachers.[20]

General rules, therefore, which limit the choice of teachers to local persons cannot be sanctioned.[21]

Criterion V

The specific requirements of any type or classification of teaching position should be definitely set up and made available for all prospective candidates.

The analysis of the functions and activities of the school positions and a careful classification of them make it possible to employ persons with the specialized skill necessary to perform the work allocated to each position.[22]

In every city the minimum eligibility requirements for each teaching position should be defined in a direct, comprehensive statement, covering (a) age, (b) academic education, (c) professional training, (d) teaching experience, and (e) other credentials required, such as certificates of birth, health, vaccination, moral character, and graduation.[23]

It is coming to be more and more recognized that the desirable kind of preparation is no longer the same for all educational positions but differs with the position sought.[24]

Criterion VI

Teachers should be selected for specific positions.

Ideally, when teachers are employed, they should be employed for a specific position in the school system. A teacher should be employed who will fit the position rather than an attempt made to fit the position to the teachers.[25]

Applications should be selected for specific positions rather than for positions in general. An occupational description for each type of work

---

[19] Graves, Frank P., *op. cit.*, p. 203.
[20] Reeder, Ward G., *op. cit.*, p. 64.
[21] *Ibid.*, p. 70.
[22] Engelhardt, Fred, *op. cit.*, p. 22.
[23] Ballou, Frank W., *op. cit.*, p. 179.
[24] Graves, Frank P., *op. cit.*, p. 181.
[25] Reeder, Ward G., *op. cit.*, p. 71.

should be in the hands of the school officer before he attempts to fill a position. Such a description is not a work sheet or job analysis but a general outline of the character of the position and the type of teacher needed.[26]

Pains should be taken to select teachers with reference to the particular position. Their qualifications should be carefully considered in the light of the type of pupils to be taught and the character of the neighborhood to be served. Such a procedure materially aids in reducing misfits to a minimum.[27]

Wise administration aims at securing a properly qualified individual for a given teaching position and protecting this position by the requirement of a specific certificate for the particular function or level of teaching.[28]

Criterion VII

Every effort should be made by those responsible for the selection of teachers to obtain complete and reliable evidence concerning the qualifications of each applicant.

When the application blank has been filled out by the candidate and has been carefully perused by the employer, if it appears that the candidate may be qualified and available, his qualifications should be further investigated.[29]

The superintendent should develop a plan whereby the qualifications of potential teachers may be accurately appraised. The following should be available for each candidate: (1) Verification of graduation from high school, including, where practical, the courses completed and the quality of record made. (2) General appraisal of quality of scholarship in institutions attended since high school graduation, including, where practical, transcripts of courses completed and marks received. (3) Specific appraisal of professional preparation for the particular type of position to which the candidate seeks appointment, records of courses completed, marks received, and letters of recommendation from key instructors. (4) Letters of recommendation covering the teaching experience of the candidate, indicating the degree of success in each position held. (5) Rating based on a systematic personal interview by one or more members of a committee responsible for preparation of lists of eligible teachers, or by other members of superintendent's staff. (6) Statement of

[26] Lewis, E. E. *Personnel Problems of the Teaching Staff*, pp. 140–141. 1925.
[27] Graves, Frank P., *op. cit.*, p. 202.
[28] National Survey of the Education of Teachers, *op. cit.*, p. 53.
[29] Reeder, Ward G., *op. cit.*, p. 68.

school physician certifying that candidate meets physical and health standards.[30]

Careful consideration of training, experience, and personal qualifications of the candidate should reduce the misfits to a minimum.[31]

Criterion VIII

A program of teacher selection should include the use of an application blank to be filled out by all candidates.

The use of application forms is a widespread practice in city systems of all sizes, and particularly so in the largest cities. . . . A formal application blank is uniform, readily filed, and easily referred to at any time.[32]

In order that information regarding the candidate's qualifications may be present in organized form, every school system should adopt a teacher's application blank which it will require all candidates to fill out. This blank should seek information upon such matters as the following: personal characteristics, training, teaching experience, type of position desired, and references.[33]

Each school system should have its own application form adapted to fit specifically the needs and purposes of the administrative organization and the rules and regulations of the local board of education.[34]

Criterion IX

Every candidate's complete credentials should include information from competent persons who are best acquainted with him and his work.

If a candidate's application is seriously considered, his qualifications should be further investigated. One well-known method of doing this is to obtain the opinions of competent persons who are acquainted with the candidate.[35]

Letters [of reference] must be secured from valid sources, that is, from persons qualified to judge the qualities of the candidate about whom they are writing.[36]

[30] *Report of the Survey of the Schools of Fort Worth, Texas*, pp. 302–303.

[31] Strayer, George D., *Official Report of the Educational Survey Commission, State of Florida*, p. 198. 1929.

[32] "Administrative Practices Affecting Classroom Teachers," *op. cit.*, p. 24.

[33] Reeder, Ward G., *op. cit.*, pp. 64, 68.

[34] Falls, J. D., "The Selection of Teachers for Classroom Instruction." *The School Board Journal*, November, 1932. p. 47.

[35] "Administrative Practices Affecting Classroom Teachers," *op. cit.*, p. 25.

[36] Brogan, Whit, *The Work of Placement Offices in Teacher Training Institutions*, p. 60. 1930.

The best forms sent to principals, supervisors, or others who have seen the candidate teach include such terms as general success in teaching, ability to maintain orderly classroom procedure, subjects or grades best fitted for, cooperative spirit, capacity for growth, general intelligence, appearance, reason for leaving position, 'would you be willing to employ,' and weakest point or points.[37]

A list of acceptable references should, of course, be included, but 'To-whom-it-may-concern' letters are practically worthless.[38]

In addition, a reference report should be sent to all of the school officials under whom and with whom the applicant has taught.[39]

Criterion X

Provision should be made in every program of teacher selection for a personal interview, where possible, with every qualified candidate.

One of the best means of securing information concerning the candidate is through the personal interview, and there are few instances when teachers should be employed without having the interview.[40]

The personal interview with candidates for teaching positions is now one of the most widely used procedures in city school systems.[41]

A personal interview has always been considered essential to a wise choice, as in that way one gains much more definite impressions than he possibly can otherwise.[42]

The oral examination, conducted by responsible administrators who must judge the effect of personality and who have the opportunity of measuring the candidates against the background of their existing staff, should be a substantial addition to the general knowledge about the candidate.[43]

The personal examination should be long enough to enable the authorities to measure the candidate properly.[44]

Many school administrators and boards of education now insist upon a personal visit by the applicant. Such a visit has its advantages for the applicant as well as for the local authorities because it permits the ap-

[37] Douglass, Harl H., *Organization and Administration of Secondary Schools*, p. 98. 1932.
[38] Maxwell, C. R. and Kilzer, L. R., *High School Administration*, p. 476. 1936.
[39] Falls, J. D., *op. cit.*, p. 47.
[40] Reeder, Ward G., *op. cit.*, p. 68.
[41] "Administrative Practices Affecting Classroom Teachers," *op. cit.*, p. 26.
[42] Graves, Frank P., *op. cit.*, p. 196.
[43] *Report of the Survey of the Schools of Chicago, Illinois*, p. 272.
[44] Cubberley, Ellwood P., *op. cit.*, p. 316.

plicant to become acquainted with the conditions under which he will be expected to teach and the persons with whom he will have to work.[45]

Criterion XI

Provision should be made in every program of teacher selection for an opportunity to observe the candidate teach.

Probably the best way of determining the teaching ability of an applicant is to observe him teach.[46]

In the last analysis, the evidence of qualifications to teach is 'demonstrated ability to teach.' . . . Probably the best means of determining the candidate's fitness to teach is to observe him teach; often this observation may be made either in the practice-teaching class in the teacher-training institution, or in the teacher's present position if he happens to be already in service.[47]

The principal will be able to judge far more effectively of the professional skill and personal qualifications of the teacher after an extended observation of the actual work in teaching situations than he can possibly do by such indirect measures as college credits, recommendations, and personal interviews.[48]

Whether he considers experienced or inexperienced applicants, he [the superintendent] will be able to visit them while they are engaged in student teaching in the training school. This method of selection is most effective and contains the smallest degree of the element of chance.[49]

Criterion XII

The certification of health and physical fitness should be a required qualification in every program of teacher selection.

Health examinations should be rated among the most important features of preparation and certification of teachers.[50]

Some of our best school systems prescribe a careful physical examination of each applicant . . . and there is a tendency to insist that certificates of health be issued only by a designated physician.[51]

[45] Maxwell, C. R. and Kilzer, L. R., *op. cit.*, p. 477.
[46] "Administrative Practices Affecting Classroom Teachers," *op. cit.*, p. 32.
[47] Reeder, Ward G., *op. cit.*, p. 69.
[48] Douglass, Harl H., *op. cit.*, p. 254.
[49] Whitney, Frederick L., *The Growth of Teachers in Service*, p. 38. 1927.
[50] Graves, Frank P., *op. cit.*, p. 184.
[51] Maxwell, C. R. and Kilzer, L. R., *op. cit.*, p. 500.

The following should be available for every candidate: statement of school physician certifying that candidate meets physical and health standards.[52]

Ten studies, reported by the American Educational Research Association, indicate the importance of physical examinations as prerequisites for teaching.[53]

The nature of the work [teaching] leads one to conclude that certain weaknesses or physical defects would be distinctly undesirable because of the psychological effect which a person who is constantly among young people may have on them.[54]

Because of the continued close contact of pupil and teacher in the classroom, there is need for assurance that the teacher is free from pulmonary and other contagious diseases. In the interests of efficiency it is also desirable to be assured that the vigor of the teacher is not impaired by constitutional physical weakness.[55]

Consideration of health demands that the teacher have good health habits.[56]

Criterion XIII

The use of the written examination as a procedure in teacher selection is very limited and need not be a necessary requirement.

In the first place examinations [written] are probably not valid tests of teaching ability. . . . Second, they are not wholly reliable.[57]

Few would defend the written examination as a sole basis for selecting and promoting teachers. . . . Even at its best, it is but one of several means of measuring and stimulating the professional growth of teachers.[58]

The trend in most states is definitely toward the graduate certificate and away from the examination system.[59]

[52] *Report of the Survey of the Schools of Fort Worth, Texas*, p. 303.
[53] Cooke, Dennis H., *Problems of the Teaching Personnel*, p. 29. 1933.
[54] Engelhardt, Fred, *op. cit.*, p. 175.
[55] Douglass, Harl H., *op. cit.*, p. 96.
[56] Foster, Herbert H., *High School Administration*, p. 71. 1928.
[57] Almack, John C. and Lang, Albert R., *Problems of the Teaching Profession*, p. 42. 1925.
[58] "Practices Affecting Teacher Personnel," *op. cit.*, p. 223.
[59] *Official Report of the Educational Survey Commission, State of Florida*, p. 188.

The written examination as a device for the selection of teachers is apparently little used by city school systems.[60]

It is likely that a wide variety of specialized written examinations is to some extent a wasteful duplication of rather elaborate means of testing the success of students which already exists in institutions from which teachers are drawn. . . . . There is a growing tendency in the direction of substitution of training credits issued by appropriate institutions.[61]

The professional tests for teachers are not substitutes for present methods of teacher selecting and rating. . . . It should be remembered that the outstanding value of such tests is relative and comparative. They give a rather accurate index of the relative standing of teachers within a group, but not the ultimate criterion of a teacher's fitness.[62]

Criterion XIV

All candidates should be required to meet approved minimum educational qualifications.

Minimum training requirements are becoming increasingly prevalent and necessary.[63]

Competent authorities in education are now generally agreed that every state and local community should set up professional training requirements which not only will protect children from unprepared teachers, but will aim to raise teacher competence to the highest possible level.[64]

There is a growing tendency in the United States to centralize full certification authority in the state departments of education.[65]

Minimum eligibility requirements . . . in each school division should be clearly defined, and the eligibility of each candidate should be determined strictly on the basis of those requirements.[66]

More and more teachers are selected with particular consideration of

[60] "Administrative Practices Affecting Classroom Teachers," *op. cit.*, p. 26.
[61] *Report of the Survey of the Schools of Chicago, Illinois*, pp. 271-272.
[62] Cooke, Dennis H., *op. cit.*, p. 209.
[63] *Ibid.*, p. 186.
[64] "Administrative Practices Affecting Classroom Teachers," *op. cit.*, p. 5.
[65] Engelhardt, Fred, *op. cit.*, p. 171.
[66] Baldwin, Clare C., *Organization and Administration of Substitute-Teaching Service in City School Systems*, p. 27. 1934.

their personal fitness and their special training for the subjects to be taught.[67]

Criterion XV

Previous teaching experience as a necessary qualification for assignment or appointment is not to be considered a uniform requirement in a program of teacher selection.

Mere years of experience without relation to type, success, and growth is of extremely doubtful value as a criterion in the selection of teachers.[68]

No accurate scale exists for evaluating the experience of teachers. Some undoubtedly continue to improve; others reach their maximum efficiency at the end of five or six years then cease to improve or actually retrograde. Another group developed the wrong teaching habits during their first year and experience only tends to increase their inefficiency.[69]

One of the fetiches of the teaching world is experience. . . . Far too high a value is commonly placed upon mere experience as such without investigating its character. The enthusiasm of an inexperienced but idealistic young teacher is a splendid tonic for both faculty and student body.[70]

But aside from the necessities and obligations of the case, it is a positive advantage to have a good minority of the staff composed of young teachers.[71]

Criterion XVI

Marriage in itself does not constitute any reasonable bar against teaching and should in no way affect the status of the candidate.

A general evaluation of the evidence seems to reveal little basis for the blanket barring of married women from teaching on the basis that they are less efficient in the classroom than single women.[72]

If a certain teacher proves to be the most satisfactory one available, her status as a married woman should not properly concern the superintend-

---

[67] Robinson, William McKinley, "Shall Untrained Persons Be Employed to Teach Our Children?" *School Life*, Vol. II, p. 59, November, 1925.

[68] Maxwell, C. R. and Kilzer, L. R., *op. cit.*, p. 499.

[69] *Official Report of the Educational Survey Commission, State of Florida*, p. 188.

[70] Foster, Herbert H., *op. cit.*, p. 75.

[71] Morgan, M. Evans and Cline, Erwin C., *Systematizing the Work of School Principals*, p. 23. 1930.

[72] "Practices Affecting Teacher Personnel," *op. cit.*, p. 221.

ent in making his selection or in retaining her. Similarly, if a divided loyalty causes her to fall below the efficiency of other teachers, she should not be chosen or kept in the system.[73]

With the lack of scientific evidence regarding the efficiency of married as compared with single women teachers, the open door policy is a wise one. Teachers should be employed and retained on the basis of efficiency.[74]

The whole problem of the married woman as a teacher can usually be solved by making a careful investigation of the probable success of the individual teacher.[75]

It is possible for discriminating school officials to select the competent married teachers from the incompetent; likewise it is possible to select the competent non-resident teacher from the incompetent. Any rule which prevents the securing of the most competent teacher is to be condemned; it is a Frankenstein.[76]

Criterion XVII

The establishment of lists of eligible candidates who have satisfactorily met all the requirements for the various types and classifications of teaching positions should be required in every program of teacher selection.

In the large city school systems the plan of selecting teachers from a merit list has been found the most practicable and successful. Eligibility lists comprise a selection from among those who have been successful in a competitive examination and have demonstrated their fitness through a personal interview conducted by a special appointment committee.[77]

The preparation of an eligible list should be influenced solely by the desire to exercise the highest possible skill in segregating from the available supply those teachers whose professional qualifications stand at the top.[78]

A rating should be given under each head according to a weighting agreed upon and the results then added together to determine the grade of each candidate. Thus an eligible list can be constructed in which the candidates are arranged in order of merit. . . . The list should, however, be good for only a year or two.[79]

[73] Graves, Frank P., *op. cit.*, p. 105.
[74] *Official Report of the Educational Survey Commission, State of Florida*, p. 197.
[75] Maxwell, C. R. and Kilzer, L. R., *op. cit.*, p. 488.
[76] Reeder, Ward G., *op. cit.*, p. 70.
[77] Engelhardt, Fred, *op. cit.*, p. 181.
[78] *Report of the Survey of the Schools of Fort Worth, Texas*, p. 304.
[79] Graves, Frank P., *op. cit.*, pp. 200-201.

Criterion XVIII

Any program of teacher selection should require a probationary period of teaching before final appointment or election.

This undergraduate period of practice is of less concern . . . than the period of probation which follows new assignments. There should be a period, extending from half to a full year, in which the beginning teacher may feel a definite and close relationship, based upon her practice in the classroom, to an established person in her school.[80]

A probationary or internship period of from two to three years needs to be developed. No final award of a certificate should be made without assurance that the person to whom it is issued possesses, over and above his academic qualifications, the ability to become proficient in the practice of his profession and the capacity for growth.[81]

Criterion XIX

Any comprehensive program of teacher selection should include a policy of selective admission or recruitment for teacher training.

Too many people are being permitted to enter teaching who have neither the native intelligence nor the social and other personal qualifications which will enable them to become successful teachers; the supply of such teachers should be stopped at the source, namely, at the entrance doors of the teacher-training institutions.[82]

There can be no effective development of a teaching staff for a school system unless its public school authorities generally on one hand and the teachers college authorities on the other share responsibility for the recruitment and selection of those who are to seek admission to the profession through the teachers college as a vestibule.[83]

The responsibility for inciting the teacher-training institutions or certificating authorities to raise certification requirements is upon the school superintendents and the large group of those who possess enough insight and influence to aid in solving the present critical condition. . . . There should be more careful pre-training selection of teacher-training candidates.[84]

[80] *Report of the Survey of the Schools of Chicago, Illinois,* Vol. I, p. 270.
[81] National Education Association, Department of Superintendence. *Fifteenth Yearbook, The Improvement of Education,* p. 149. 1937.
[82] Reeder, Ward G., *op. cit.,* p. 152.
[83] Suhrie, Ambrose L., "The Superintendent of Schools and the Education of Teachers." *Official Report,* Department of Superintendence of the National Education Association, Atlantic City, N. J., 1935, pp. 204–205.
[84] Cooke, Dennis H., *op. cit.,* pp. 17–18.

A canvass of leading educators made by the 1935 Yearbook Commission of the Department of Superintendence indicates a strong sentiment in favor of limiting those admitted to teacher-preparatory institutions to those who rank in the upper third of their high school classes. . . . In addition to a broad cultural foundation, individuals who intend to prepare for teaching should give evidence that they possess the necessary qualities of character, emotional fitness, and health to serve as leaders for the youth of today before we admit them to our teacher-training institutions.[85]

These nineteen criteria are set up as a measure for the evaluation of administrative procedures in teacher selection. Authoritative documentary evidence, current practices, and trends in school administration give validity and merit to these underlying principles which should form the bases of any comprehensive program planned to secure and maintain a strong, highly efficient teaching personnel.

[85] Potter, Milton C., in *Official Report* of the Department of Superintendence, 1935, p. 202.

CHAPTER III

ORGANIZATION FOR ADMINISTERING THE PROGRAM OF TEACHER SELECTION

THE RESPONSIBILITY OF THE SUPERINTENDENT OF SCHOOLS FOR SELECTION OF TEACHERS

THE most outstanding fact established in school administration is the responsibility of the superintendent of schools and the authority vested in that executive officer for the selection of teachers. The function of initiating appointments or assignments through proper recommendations to the board of education has been delegated to the superintendent in recognition of the fact that the selection of teachers is an important professional and technical matter, and that his ability and special training prepare him to judge the qualifications and fitness of candidates for teaching positions. Moreover, it is recognized that efficiency is best maintained by holding the superintendent responsible for the selection of the teaching personnel whose work he is to supervise and for whose results he is to be held responsible. Accordingly, the initiative in all matters relative to the nomination for appointment or assignment of teachers rests with the superintendent of schools.[1]

A study of the practices of the thirty-seven school systems investigated reveals that in thirty-five of them the ultimate responsibility for the selection of teachers definitely rests with the superintendent and that their boards of education have specifically delegated this administrative function to the executive head of the school system. This delegation of responsibility is clearly indicated in statements taken from the rules and regulations of the boards of education or from their administrative codes, a few examples of which follow:

All elections and appointments shall be made upon the recommendation of the Superintendent.

The initiative in all matters relating to the appointment and assignment

[1] Criterion I, p. 12.

of teachers shall rest with the Superintendent of Schools; and all applicants for such positions shall be referred to him.

The Superintendent shall appoint all assistants to the Superintendent, directors, assistant directors, supervisors, assistant supervisors, principals, teachers, assistant teachers, and attendance officers.

The Superintendent shall have sole power to nominate all Assistant Superintendents, supervisors, principals, teachers, and other employees of the Board of Education.

These statements are representative of special provisions whereby the responsibility of teacher selection has been centered in the office of the school executive in thirty-five of the cities. In the other two cities a slightly different interpretation can be placed on the procedure followed, but even in these two cases the superintendent is influential and exercises a direct or indirect approval. In New York City there is a Board of Examiners, selected by the Municipal Civil Service Commission from among those who have taken a competitive examination, appointed by the Board of Education, and independent of the superintendent's office. This Board of Examiners examines all candidates and determines their eligibility. All selections to positions in the school system must be made from an eligible list prepared by this Board. Because of its size and complex organization, this city system is an exception to the policy followed throughout the state. During the past year the Legislature of New York has realized the importance of the proper placement of this responsibility with the superintendent of schools and has incorporated the following as part of the Education Law:

District superintendents, directors, supervisors, principals, teachers, and all other members of the teaching and supervisory staff, except associate superintendents and examiners, shall be appointed by the board of education, upon the recommendation of the superintendent of schools, but in a city having a board of superintendents, on the recommendation of such board.[2]

In Dallas, Texas, the Board of Education has placed this function of teacher selection with the assistant superintendent as follows:

The Assistant Superintendent of Schools shall be elected at the same time and for the same term as the Superintendent of Schools.

[2] State of New York, *Education Law*, Article 33-A, Section 872, in effect May 23, 1936.

The Assistant Superintendent of Schools shall at all times be in direct charge of the teaching corps, and shall be immediately responsible for the administration of the schools.

He shall select and recommend to the Board, as needed, a sufficient number of qualified teachers, properly and adequately prepared to carry on the work of instruction, and, subject to the approval of the Superintendent of Schools, shall make the allotment and assignment of teachers to the various schools.[3]

Apparently the function has been delegated in these two systems by their respective boards of education to other school officials specially trained and selected for the purpose. However, the superintendents, as executive officers of their boards, can and do advise concerning the formulation of the principles and policies governing their programs of teacher selection.

In practice, then, the superintendent is held responsible for the selection of teachers. He nominates and the basis of his endorsement is open to inspection at any time. This procedure demands cooperation between the board of education and its executive office, and recognizes the ability and training of the superintendent to judge the qualifications and fitness of candidates for teaching positions. Thus, Strayer advises that "the responsibilities for all personnel recommendations and all aspects of administration having to do with the personnel employed by the Board of Education should be centered in the office of the superintendent of schools."[4] Members of boards of education, rarely trained for this important responsibility, should adopt the standards and qualifications of teachers they wish to employ in their systems under the prevailing salary scale, and then delegate the responsibility of rating the candidates and making nominations to the superintendent.

This Responsibility of the Superintendent Is a Most Important One

The instructional effectiveness in any school system is limited by its staff of teachers. Newlon says, "As far as schools are concerned, the actual progress of education is almost completely in the hands of

[3] Dallas Public Schools, *Rules and Regulations*, Section III, Articles 10, 11, and 12, p. 14.
[4] *Report of the Survey of the Schools of Chicago, Illinois*, Vol. I, p. 92.

the million classroom teachers of the country." [5] The best service can be expected only from properly trained and well-qualified teachers. Since every child has the right to be well educated and is entitled to the best teachers available, the schools entrusted with the care and instruction of children should be staffed by competent teachers. Thus every procedure in the superintendent's program for teacher selection must provide for the elimination of the unfit or unprepared by careful selection at every step in the process.

There are many factors which help to determine the fitness of teachers and which should be considered by the superintendent and his staff. Such factors are general training, specific training, professional training, teaching experience, health, age, character, and personality. Many important procedures are also involved in any acceptable program of teacher selection. The establishment of adequate sources of candidates, securing the necessary data on candidates, the activities of the candidates in presenting their complete applications, the methods of evaluating credentials, the establishment of eligibles, and the assignment or appointment of those best qualified are all important steps. Surely, to meet the demands of this administrative function, the responsibility of the superintendent becomes a very important one.

This Responsibility of the Superintendent Carries with It the Obligation to Secure the Best Teachers Possible with the Available Income of the Community

Believing in the principle that both state and federal funds for education should be made available, if necessary, in order that every school community may have an equal opportunity to secure competent teachers, the writer realizes that local salary schedules and local requirements at the present time make it possible for some school systems to demand higher qualifications, longer experience, better preparation, and to secure more efficient teachers than other systems. Nevertheless, regardless of the local situation each superintendent should keep in mind one question when selecting teachers for his schools: "Is she or he the best possible candidate available for the

[5] Newlon, Jesse H., *Educational Administration as Social Policy*. Part III: Report of the Commission on the Social Studies, American Historical Association, p. 170. 1934.

position?" As Cubberley has stated, "For every position the most efficient teacher that the system can employ under its salary schedule should be secured." [6]

The boards of education in twenty-six of the cities represented in this study, realizing the justification of this basic principle, have incorporated in their "rules and regulations" or "administrative codes" definite instructions to their executive officers that they select only the best possible candidates. Several examples of these instructions are indicative of the practice:

> In making the first appointment to a position in the Denver Schools, the Superintendent of Schools and his associates will consider only the welfare of the boys and girls in the schools. From the list of available candidates, the best fitted persons will be chosen, training, experience, character, and personality considered. The sole purpose will be to serve the schools. (Denver)

> The initial appointment of any person to any type of position shall be made solely for the purpose of providing the best available service for the schools. In making selection among several possible candidates, consideration of comparable fitness to render the best service shall determine each case of first appointment. (Minneapolis)

> The initial appointment of any person to any type of position shall be made solely for the purpose of providing the best available service for the schools. The interests or needs of the candidate seeking a first appointment, the mere length of experience, the mere fact of former employment in the schools, or the place of residence of such candidate shall not be considered as qualifications for or as claims upon appointment. (Cleveland)

While no such explicit statements are to be found in the regulations of the other eleven systems, there are evidences of implied responsibility to select the best available candidates permitted under the local conditions.

This Responsibility of the Superintendent Carries with It the Obligation to Base the Program of Teacher Selection upon Merit

Skilled teaching demands a trained, competent teaching personnel. This is particularly true if teaching is to be made, kept, and popularly understood as professional work requiring special preparation

---

[6] Cubberley, Ellwood P., *Public School Administration*, p. 308. 1929.

and technical competence and dedicated to the development and growth of children. Every community should place its schools above selfish, petty, and political influence and should build around its system of education a strong popular feeling of pride, ethics, and child interest which no job hunter, no social group, no money power, no political pressure can thrust aside and rob its children of the best teachers available.

No branch of any city service should be considered primarily an employment service. The teaching service, in particular, should be organized and administered so that it will attract the best qualified candidates, and the system of selecting such candidates should be based upon merit.[7] Quoting from the National Survey of the Education of Teachers: "State and national campaigns of education should be conducted to encourage school-board members to select new teachers upon the basis of scholarship, special professional preparation, experience, and merit, rather than upon such bases as local residence, willingness to accept lower salaries, and similar factors." [8] All who are interested in the teaching profession should endeavor to educate the public school communities to select only the best trained teachers from among all the available candidates and to base that selection on merit.

The boards of education and the school executives in the cities represented in this survey have stressed this basic principle in teacher selection in their rules and regulations or in announcements made available both to the public and to candidates for teaching positions. Four examples of such statements illustrate this policy:

The employment of any sort of personal, political or social influence to secure appointment to the teaching force, or the urging of any consideration other than fitness for the work of teaching, as a ground for such appointment is held to be an act of unprofessional conduct and is strictly forbidden. (Los Angeles)

The rules of the Board of Education require that all appointments and promotions of teachers shall be made upon the basis of merit, to be ascertained as far as practicable, in cases of appointment, by examination or other evidence of preparation and experience; and in cases of promotion by length and character of service. (St. Louis)

[7] Criterion II, p. 13.   [8] National Survey of the Education of Teachers, Vol. II: *Teacher Personnel in the United States*, p. 104.

The use of any personal or political influence or the urging of any factor other than professional fitness shall be regarded as unprofessional conduct which shall warrant the Superintendent to refuse to further consider an applicant for a teaching position. (Oakland)

In the appointment and continuance of the teaching staff, the Superintendent of Schools shall especially consider superior qualifications as to moral character, industry, educational and professional attainments and practical skill in instruction and school management. (Indianapolis)

The choice of a teacher should be absolutely a professional matter and any program of teacher selection should be based upon merit.[9] Undoubtedly there is complete agreement with the criterion on the part of all the thirty-seven cities. It is an accepted policy, and, to all intent and purposes, is followed in actual practice. However, only a detailed examination of all the procedures that are involved can determine the value of the merit basis in teacher selection in any system.

THE ORGANIZATION FOR ADMINISTERING THE PROGRAM OF TEACHER SELECTION

An efficient program of teacher selection demands some type of organization responsible for the activities having to do with personnel management.[10] Since the superintendent of schools is not only the executive officer of his board of education but also the professional leader of the instructional, business, and building programs of his system, it becomes imperative that he be able to delegate some of his powers and duties to subordinate supervisory and administrative assistants. Because of the many problems and details directly related to teacher selection, and in order to carry through to a successful conclusion the various procedures involved, some type of organization is necessary. In the thirty-seven cities included in this study, most of the boards of education and school superintendents have, in one way or another, endeavored to meet this need. For example, some cities, such as New York, Jersey City, Newark, and Washington, have established "boards of examiners." In Cleveland one finds a "bureau of personnel" and in Pittsburgh a "personnel department." Philadelphia has its "division of examinations" with a director in

[9] Criterion II, p. 13.
[10] Criterion III, p. 14.

charge; San Francisco, a "department of personnel"; Rochester, a department of "teacher employment and certification." Indianapolis, Baltimore, and Providence have the direction of teacher examinations under the department of research. In Milwaukee the Board of School Directors has its "committee on examinations and appointments." This committee instructs the superintendent of schools and his assistants to conduct examinations of teachers and to present the results of such examinations for its inspection and action, subject to the approval of the board. Kansas City with its "examining board," Seattle with its "committee of raters," and Cincinnati with its "director of personnel" represent other types of organizations in charge of teacher selection. In other cities where no special name or title has been assigned to such organization, committees composed of the superintendent and designated members of his supervisory, administrative, teaching, and clerical staffs function as selecting agencies. These variations in existing types of organization concerned with teacher selection are summarized in Table III.

TABLE III

TYPES OF ORGANIZATIONS IN CHARGE OF TEACHER SELECTION
IN 37 CITIES

	Number of Cities
Board of Examiners	8
Division of Examinations (or Department)	4
Personnel Department (or Bureau)	6
Department of Research	3
Committee on Examinations and Appointment	4
Department of Teacher Employment and Certification	1
Superintendent's Committee	11

The organization of these various administrative subdivisions and committees differs considerably in both personnel and duties according to the size and type of the local school system. In New York City the Board of Examiners is composed of seven members. These members meet definite qualifications, take competitive examinations, are appointed from an eligible list, and hold tenure of office. In Pittsburgh the administration of matters pertaining to personnel in the public schools is placed by the superintendent of schools in the hands of the associate superintendent of schools in charge of personnel. In Philadelphia the Division of Examinations consists of a director, an assistant director, a special assistant, and seven clerical assistants. For the various examinations given from time to time, the assistance of superintendents, directors, principals, heads of departments, and other members of the supervisory staff of the system is secured. The superintendent of schools is chairman ex-officio of all examining committees. In Detroit the Personnel Committee is composed of nine members—the assistant superintendent in charge of teacher personnel, the assistant superintendent in charge of intermediate and high schools, the assistant superintendent in charge of finance, the supervisory director of instruction, the supervisory director of intermediate schools, the director of statistics and publications, the director of assignments and transfers of teachers in elementary schools, and two elementary school principals, one being a district principal. The Board of Examiners of Jersey City is composed of the superintendent of schools and six persons of "lawful requirement" appointed by the Board of Education. In Denver the Examining Board is composed of only five members. They include the assistant superintendent as chairman, the deputy superintendent in charge of high schools, the assistant superintendent in charge of elementary schools, and two principals. In Chicago the Board of Examiners has consisted of the superintendent together with two other members approved and appointed by the Board of Education, upon the recommendation of its officer. In the Chicago survey report of 1932 a different organization was suggested, and it was recommended that the members of the board of examiners be chosen from a list of trained specialists whose eligibility should be determined by examinations set up by qualified professional leaders outside the immediate staff of the city school system. It was further recommended that, as a result of these examinations, a list of eligibles be prepared, each person being rated in order of fitness and qualifications, and the list furnished to the Board of Education. The examiners, three in number, were to be selected from this list by the Board of Education; and the recommendations carried the further stipulation that the three highest, in the order in which they are rated, be selected. [11]

[11] *Report of the Survey of the Schools of Chicago, Illinois,* Vol. I, pp. 23–24.

Functions of Selecting Agencies

Regardless of the type of organization, these selecting agencies have certain definite functions which are necessary in the field of personnel selection. A detailed study of the prescribed functions of the agencies in the larger cities indicated that three types of activities are involved: (1) obtaining the best possible teachers, (2) providing for their professional growth, and (3) providing conditions which will insure at all times that they will do their best teaching.

In Philadelphia the following work is assigned to the Division of Examinations: [12]

1. Preparation of eligible lists, including
    (*a*) Evaluation of credentials.
    (*b*) Examination of applicants for
        (1) Entrance to the system.
        (2) Promotion within the system.
        (3) Reappointment to the system.

2. State certification, including
    (*a*) Records of teachers employed by the Board of Public Education and of applicants for positions.
    (*b*) Extension and renewal of certificates, and conversion of temporary certificates to permanent certificates.

3. Personnel accounting.

The functions of the Bureau of Personnel in Cleveland are definitely stated as follows:

1. To receive, classify and file for use all applications for teaching positions in the Cleveland schools.

2. To ascertain and verify the formal educational qualifications and teaching records of all such applicants, and evaluate them according to the standards prescribed for entrance in the Cleveland school system.

3. To arrange and keep such information so as to be conveniently available for the use of the superintendent and his assistants in selecting teachers for appointment.

4. To keep such information concerning teachers in the Cleveland service as the superintendent may require for use in considering promotions and transfers of teachers within the system.

[12] School District of Philadelphia, The Board of Public Education. *Division of Examinations: Report,* June 30, 1931, p. 9.

5. To pass upon the educational qualifications of all teachers as the basis of administering the salary schedules.

6. To receive requests from principals of schools for substitutes for teachers who may fail to meet their classes, to communicate promptly with suitably qualified substitutes who have been appointed to teach such classes, and to procure their services in such cases.

7. To keep such records as may be needed for use in determining what services have been rendered by substitutes in the school.[13]

The Personnel Department in the city of St. Louis has been assigned the following activities:

1. To receive all applications for appointment to positions in the department of instruction, to write to references, to collect all personnel data for intelligent interpretation of applications, to score the applications in accordance with the scoring plan approved by the Superintendent of Instruction, to compile record of scores for reference, and to keep a complete file of the applications and accompanying data.

2. To study available applications in relation to vacancies existing and to report to the superintendent in proper form the qualifications possessed by applicants with reference to these positions.

3. To interview all candidates who call in person and secure from them in writing all information necessary for considering their cases.

4. To conduct all preliminary examinations of applicants and arrange for visiting applicants for the oral examination.[14]

In Pittsburgh all matters pertaining to teacher selection in the public schools are placed by the superintendent of schools in the hands of the associate superintendent of schools in charge of personnel, who is definitely assigned the following functions, under the direction of the superintendent of schools and with the approval of the Board:

1. To develop an organization and the necessary technique for the purpose of determining where and by whom superior service is being rendered, so that the provisions for rewarding conspicuously high grade service as provided for in the various salary schedules can become operative.

2. To use his organization in cooperation with other administrative departments and with supervisors and principals for the early develop-

---

[13] *Administrative Code of the Cleveland School Board*, Section 232, pp. 24–25.

[14] Board of Education, St. Louis, Missouri, *Annual Report of the Superintendent of Instruction*, p. 17. 1927.

ment of superior teachers during the automatic increment years of the teacher's experience.

3. To make specific recommendations for the advancement of such personnel who are rendering superior service and who have met the necessary requirements, to the salary levels provided in the schedules.

4. To give direction to the training of teachers and principals in service who aspire to qualify for the superior service levels. Such direction necessarily must include both the nature of the training pursued, and the amount of such training as a teacher may be permitted to carry at any one time. This provision will properly tend to protect the health of the teacher and to prevent a lowering of the quality of classroom instruction.

5. To develop a program for the selection of new teachers brought into the system. The Personnel Department should stimulate the enlistment of the finest of recruits to the teaching service.

6. To recommend to the Superintendent of Schools the appointment, the transfer, and the demotion of teachers; and the dismissal of personnel whose services are manifestly unsatisfactory.

7. To develop under the direction of the Superintendent of Schools a program in connection with the Frick Training School for the proper selection of high school graduates for admission to the Frick Training School, and to assume jointly with the Frick Training School and the Department of Curriculum Study responsibility for the improvement of the curriculum of that institution.

8. To develop and operate a system of personnel records for the entire school system which will be cumulative and comprehensive.[15]

The Board of Examiners of New York City have their functions listed as follows:

1. To test the fitness of applicants for all
    a. Teaching positions.
    b. Supervisory positions (with a few exceptions).
    c. School clerical positions.
    d. Compulsory Education Law enforcement officer positions.

2. To certify to the Superintendent of Schools for the issuance of licenses the names of those found qualified.

While these general functions are so designated, it is interesting to

[15] Pittsburgh Public Schools, *Report of Committee on Finance and Administration,* December 23, 1929, pp. 17–18.

note that in the Annual Report of the School Department of New York City for 1930 the following work of the examiners is listed:

1. Interview candidates.
2. Prepare or revise examination papers.
3. Read or re-read examination papers.
4. Watch the progress of an examination from the time of the preparation of the circular through
   (*a*) Preparation of the list.
   (*b*) Construction of the examination paper.
   (*c*) Selection of assistant examiners.
   (*d*) Re-reading for both content and English.
   (*e*) Giving the interview examination.
   (*f*) Re-examination.
5. Check up on what is being done on each examination each week.
6. Attend weekly meetings of the Board of Examiners.
7. Make reports on special subjects.
8. Make special investigations of doubtful records of candidates.
9. Prepare special examination questions.
10. Prepare standard answer sheet or keys.
11. Make improvements from time to time in the procedures.
12. Attend to office correspondence.

In the city of Denver the examining board is appointed by the superintendent to (1) meet applicants, (2) examine credentials, and (3) recommend for the eligible list. While these three functions describe in general terms the work of the examining board, the following specific duties are listed in the system's procedure in making appointments to teaching positions in the city's schools:

1. To interview each applicant.
2. To form an estimate of the applicant's personal qualifications independently of the estimate made by other members.
3. To meet as a body and examine the credentials of each applicant.
4. To write for recommendations from references named by the applicant.
5. To obtain other necessary information about the applicant.
6. To examine the applicant by means of two brief formal examinations, a general information test and an English composition test.

7. To decide by vote as to whether the individual shall be recommended for the eligible list. A majority vote of the examining board in approval recommends him to the deputy superintendent.

In New Jersey the Board of Examiners is given the power to grant certificates; to revoke licenses granted by the Board, for cause, after a hearing; to hold examinations; and to prepare eligible lists.

In other cities where the detailed duties of the selecting agencies are not definitely set forth in either printed or mimeographed form, the writer found, by means of personal interview or correspondence, that the following duties were mentioned most frequently:

1. Establishing qualifications for the various teaching positions.

2. Preparing forms to be used in the program of teacher selection: circulars of information, application blanks, form letters, notices of interviews, examinations, etc.

3. Examining credentials and recommendations.

4. Corresponding with teacher-training institutions and colleges and references in order to ascertain, verify, and collect all records.

5. Classifying and filing for convenient use all applications and information regarding each applicant.

6. Interviewing applicants.

7. Preparing examination papers where needed.

8. Arranging for written examinations and practical tests where required.

9. Observing classroom teaching of applicants.

10. Conducting examinations and arranging for their proper marking or rating.

11. Preparing graded eligible lists, lists of successful candidates, or lists of satisfactory or qualified applicants.

12. Keeping up to date the academic and professional record of teachers in service.

13. Developing with the local normal school or teacher-training institution a program for the proper selection of high school graduates for admission to such institutions.

While this study does not undertake to establish the separate duties of the selecting agency at this point, the practices and procedures which are presented and discussed in the later chapters and the recommendations concerning each will indicate the scope of those duties as applied to the selection of teachers. Nevertheless, the delegation of duties by the superintendent to the selecting agency carries with it the same obligation to secure the best teachers possible and to base the program of selection solely upon merit.

SUMMARY AND CONCLUSIONS

The importance of the problem of teacher selection and the complexity of the activities involved demand some type of organization or selecting agency. Because of the ever-present pressure of non-educational groups, political favoritism and interference, social power, and other unfortunate influences, it is desirable that this agency be immediately responsible to the superintendent and that it take a strictly professional attitude toward its duties. The size and comprehensiveness of the school system may determine the size of the selecting agency, the method of its appointment, and, in part, its type of organization; nevertheless, certain outstanding requirements and standards must be professionally met and adequately satisfied in order that it may function in the way that good administration and trends in practice recommend. They are:

1. The members of the selecting agency shall be those best qualified for the important work of teacher selection.

2. The selecting agency shall have access to the expert opinion and assistance of specialists in the various classified positions.

3. The agency must be free from the pressure of non-educational groups, political, social, fraternal, or church; and from unscrupulous or selfish individual influence.

4. Its organization and operation must be such that it will be possible to establish, as best it can, qualifications and measurements of a type that will promise satisfactory protection against charges of favoritism and influence of any non-professional character.

5. Its organization and operation shall be so planned that it functions effectively in the selection of the best qualified and the elimination of the unfit or undesirable teachers.

These recommendations are basic if the agency is to function efficiently. Moreover, they are in keeping with the general criteria underlying sound administrative practices in the selection of teachers.

PART II

Administrative Practices Used in the Selection of Teachers

CHAPTER IV

RECRUITING THE CANDIDATES

THE SOURCES OF DESIRABLE TEACHERS

ANY program established for the selection of teachers of necessity must consider the several sources to which school systems can turn for desirable teachers. Although it is a well-recognized principle in school administration that such teachers should be sought,[1] few of the large city systems have the opportunity or find the time to make a definite, active search for desirable candidates to fill available positions in the schools. Where the system maintains its own teacher-training institution, local statutory regulations will sometimes restrict, to a large extent, the sources. For example, in New Orleans the following regulation controls the situation in part:

> In recommending applicants for vacancies in the elementary grades of the white schools, preference shall be given to graduates of New Orleans Normal School. When the list of New Orleans Normal Graduates is exhausted, preference will be given to those possessing teaching experience and bachelor or master degrees from approved colleges.

In St. Louis all positions as teachers in the elementary schools are filled by the appointment of graduates of the Teachers College maintained by the Board of Education in the city of St. Louis for the training of elementary teachers. A similar situation exists in Detroit where holders of certificates or diplomas from the Detroit Teachers College are eligible for appointment as probationary teachers in the elementary schools, and upon the satisfactory completion of the probationary period of one year shall be ranked as regular teachers.

In the systems where written examinations are held, the boards of education are required by law to have printed in the local newspapers notice of such examinations. These notices are usually included in school bulletins as well, so that members of the supervisory and teaching staffs are made cognizant of the examinations and can, di-

[1] Criterion IV, p. 14.

rectly or indirectly, advertise the fact. In addition, most of these cities keep a mailing list of all chance applicants during the period between examinations and send out individual notices just before the next examinations are to be held. A few of the largest systems send out notices of teachers' examinations to all teacher-training institutions and colleges within certain areas. For example, the Board of Examiners of the New York City system recently sent notices to all such institutions in New York, New Jersey, Connecticut, and parts of Pennsylvania. One member of this same board visited during the past year superintendents and principals in other systems, soliciting their aid in getting desirable teachers to take the examinations.

All the cities keep more or less systematic files of applications from acceptably qualified candidates, but in most cases the applications are the result of chance. Some few of the cities, however, try in other ways to have available highly desirable candidates for possible vacancies. Eleven cities reported following up, from time to time, chance information concerning outstanding work by teachers in other systems. Six cities reported attempts to secure applications from outstanding teachers recommended on request. For example, in Cincinnati the director of personnel sends out at stated times a form letter to various teacher-training institutions and to educational leaders within as well as outside the state. This letter reads in part:

> Will you kindly nominate, for appointment consideration, two or three outstanding successful teachers—recent graduates of a four-year training course, who have had at least two years of successful teaching experience? We are looking for earnest young people whose training and experience have given them a maturity in professional activity and a mastery of the special field.
>
> Please do not notify candidates of a possible vacancy here. Credentials from your Bureau of Appointment will be given consideration first. The initial approach of the formal application should come from this office.

The type of teaching position and the special subject field are indicated in the letter. The recommendations and credentials are evaluated and those considered most desirable are marked for visitation and interview if they are interested. The individuals whose recommendations are so honored receive a letter from the office of the superintendent, which reads in part:

At the suggestion of ——————————, we are writing to inquire if you would care to submit an application for a position in our schools. If you are interested in securing a position in our schools and if you meet substantially the qualifications for appointment, statement of which is enclosed, please fill out the application blank in detail and forward it, together with an official transcript of your credits.

This procedure is to be commended. It not only reduces very considerably the number of unfit or poorly prepared candidates, but it also makes possible an ever ready source of highly desirable candidates with varied experiences and backgrounds. Moreover, this practice can be carried on through the year, and hurried decisions can be avoided.

No evidence was found that any of the cities considered in the study used the commercial teachers' agencies as a source of teacher supply. In fact two cities, Los Angeles and Portland, definitely state in their "Information to Applicants" blanks the following:

No teachers' agency can give you assistance whatever in securing a position in the —————————— School District. To seek help from that source will prove unavailing.

The chance receipt of applications plays a large part in determining the source of available teachers in many of the cities. The desirable salary schedules and the opportunity to continue professional studies in the larger institutions, so frequently located in or near these cities, bring forth applications in practically every mail. Usually there is no vacancy at the time, so a form acknowledgment is mailed to the applicant, such as the following:

We beg to advise you that your application with reference to a position has been received. So far as can be judged at the present time, there will be (or is) no vacancy in the line of work for which you make aplication.

In case of a future vacancy for which you may be qualified, we shall be pleased to communicate with you.

Unless there is a careful and continuous evaluation and elimination of such applications, the files become stocked with hundreds of chance applications which, when the time comes to fill a vacancy, have too often imposed limitations on any other sources of desirable candidates. To correct this situation, most of the cities invalidate the applications after a period of one, two, or three years and remove them from the files. In addition, some of the cities notify the "would be" applicant at the time the request for an application blank is made that there are no vacancies. The following form letter used in Kansas City illustrates the practice:

> There are no vacancies in the public schools of this city at the present time. It seems there will be few, if any, vacancies for the next year or additional teachers needed.
>
> In our files are more than two thousand applications. Most of these applicants are graduates of teachers' colleges or universities—many of them with Master's degrees. We have personally interviewed several hundred of these applicants. Some have very high testimonials but cannot be employed because we have no place for them.
>
> It seems useless for us to receive more applications and for you to spend the time and money to present yourself for personal interview. Unless you come for such an interview, it is useless for you to apply.
>
> We are enclosing blanks, but advise against filing them.

There is, however, sufficient evidence in the reports of administrative and personnel officers for the claim that more and more they are turning to appointment and placement bureaus in normal schools, colleges, and universities for desirable candidates. This is as it should be. Such teacher-training institutions are by far the most important source of teacher supply.[2] According to Brogan, the placement bureaus of teacher-training institutions are effective agencies for furnishing information about teachers. They are not only concerned with the placement of young people who are about to be graduated or who have recently been graduated, but equally interested in giving valuable assistance to former graduates who wish to secure positions elsewhere.[3] At the same time, school systems should avoid selecting a preponderance of any teaching staff from a small number of institutions. The vivifying influence that comes from selecting teachers with varying backgrounds, both academic and professional, is most desirable.

---

[2] Madsen, I. N., "The Predicting of Teaching Success." *Educational Administration and Supervision*, January, 1927, p. 47.

[3] Brogan, Whit, *The Work of Placement Offices in Teacher-Training Institutions*, p. 77.

Local Candidates

During the past five years, the tendency in most of the largest cities has been to give preference to local residents and to graduates of local institutions in making initial assignments or appointments. The reasons given are: "economic conditions in the community," "helping the unemployment situation," and "taking care of our own first." In every case the practice was deemed necessary in view of the local situation. Nevertheless, while there may be justifiable reasons for such local preference in times of great economic distress, sound administration practices will heed the dangers of too much in-breeding, will consider its effect upon the school system, and will take the necessary precautions to keep a professional balance. Strayer and Engelhardt state, "The dangers of restricting intellectual and professional growth to local influences are so great as to indicate the desirability of a policy of taking at all times a certain number of teachers both experienced and inexperienced from outside the city If the numbers in the normal college are limited to a small percentage below the expected requirements of the elementary schools and if applicants are encouraged from other sources, the resulting variety of experience should be a great benefit to the schools." [4] Moreover, Graves believes that it would be well to place some limit upon the number of home teachers to be permitted in any school system, even when their competency is fully equal to that of the best candidates from outside.[5] The 'question involved concerns itself primarily with the selection of the best qualified candidate that is available for the position. All sources of supply should be tapped and every effort made to seek desirable candidates.

Summary and Conclusions

No school system should depend either upon its own local supply of applicants or upon the chance receipt of applications or inquiring letters from those interested in securing teaching positions. While there is no evidence to support any definite percentage of local teachers, administrative and personnel officers should endeavor to limit the percentage to a reasonable proportion in order to avoid any ex-

[4] *Report of the Survey of the Schools of Chicago, Illinois,* Vol. I, p. 259.
[5] Graves, Frank P., *Public School Organization and Administration,* p. 194.

cessive or harmful "in-breeding" and to give the schools the benefit of broader experience, wider educational viewpoints, and worthy outside practices. Moreover, where local charter provisions or state regulations may designate graduates of certain institutions or holders of state certificates as eligible for teaching positions, there should be no legislation to prevent boards of education and their agencies from seeking elsewhere for desirable candidates who can satisfactorily meet the standard or certifying qualifications. The two best sources for such candidates are other school systems and the placement bureaus in teacher-training institutions.

INFORMATION TO PROSPECTIVE CANDIDATES

The specific requirements of any type or classification of teaching position should be definitely set up and made available for all prospective candidates.[6] Teachers are to be selected for specific positions [7] which often demand special qualifications. In order that candidates may be well qualified, they should have available all necessary information concerning the special as well as the general requirements of the position for which application is to be made. Such information, if definitely planned and made available, will not only encourage those to apply who are particularly well fitted for the position but also decrease considerably the number of general applications of those not specially qualified. Selecting agencies must be well acquainted with the different types or classifications of teaching positions and must know what each requires by way of special, professional, and general training, experience, physical requirements, and working conditions involved.

Circulars of Information

To bring this information to prospective candidates, school systems use various types of form letters or circulars of information. Of the thirty-seven cities represented in this study, twenty-six use an "Information for Applications" form or circular which usually accompanies the application blank. In the very largest cities, especially where written examinations are held, these circulars of information

---

[6] Criterion V, p. 15.   [7] Criterion VI, p. 15.

are quite elaborate, giving not only the usual information concerning requirements and necessary qualifications but also detailed information about the examinations and their scope. In the smaller cities the circulars are very limited in their informational material and could very well be incorporated in the general application blank. In fact, the eleven cities not using these circulars do include such necessary information in the application blank.

Most of the circulars of information are in printed form, although a few cities are using mimeographed material. The circulars vary in form and size from a four-page folder, eight inches by twelve inches, to a single sheet, three inches by six inches.

The type of information included in these circulars differs considerably from city to city, according to the regulations and procedures governing teacher selection. Most of the circulars give the prospective candidate sufficient detailed information concerning eligibility requirements and the necessary procedures to follow if one wishes to apply for a position. Table IV shows the nine most frequently listed items about which specific information is given to candidates.

TABLE IV

ITEMS ABOUT WHICH INFORMATION WAS MOST FREQUENTLY
GIVEN IN CIRCULARS OF INFORMATION

Items	Number of Cities
General information, including such items as age requirements, citizenship, medical certification, verification of education and experience, etc.	26
Qualifications or requirements.	26
Personal interview.	26
Certification or teaching certificates.	18
Directions for filling out and returning application blank.	17
Eligible list, preferred or ranking list.	16
Examinations, including such items as time, place, nature or scope, subjects, regulations, etc.	11
Salary schedule, salary regulations.	11
Teachers Retirement Law or Retirement Fund Association.	10

Other informational material found in the circulars of a few cities dealt with: duties of teachers, residence within city, rules relating to the payment of salaries, married women or marriage, rates for board and room in the community, successful vaccination, and date of election or appointment.

Practice among these large cities tends toward the continued use of circulars of information to candidates. Such informational material serves three major purposes: (1) to act as a self-measuring or rating scale so that the prospective candidate can determine her fitness in terms of the eligibility requirements; (2) to give explicit directions to the candidate concerning successive procedures to follow in qualifying for assignment or appointment; and (3) to give information to teacher-training institutions so that their students can be prepared to meet the requirements for a teaching position. The form and the scope of the circular of information will, of necessity, differ according to the local situation. However, certain standards should apply in their use and composition. The circular of information has a definite place in a program of teacher selection and should be:

1. Available to all who are interested in becoming applicants.
2. Available to all teacher-training institutions which may be interested in supplying candidates.
3. Carefully worded and logically arranged so that it may be readily comprehended.
4. Definite as to qualifications necessary.
5. Definite as to requirements and regulations governing the necessary procedures to be followed by the applicant.
6. Informative regarding the prevalent salary schedule.

These standards are necessary if circulars of information are to serve their purpose. It is of first importance that they definitely check the further application of those who cannot qualify and those who will not be interested in what the position offers. The circular of information will be valuable in a program of teacher selection only to the degree that it makes this self-checking effective.

SECURING INFORMATION CONCERNING QUALIFICATIONS OF APPLICANTS

Those responsible for the selection of teachers are obligated to ascertain the fitness of all applicants and to determine, as far as possible, the relative merits of each. This demands complete, reliable information concerning the qualifications of all who apply.[8] Such information must be obtained through reliable sources and by uniform practices which cannot be criticized because of unfairness, incompleteness, or lack of proper certification or verification. Every requirement must be satisfied by the applicant if he is to be considered for the position; and the selecting agency is responsible for the collection of all data concerning the applicant and for the verification of all records. This procedure involves complete and reliable evidence of training, experience, health, age, character, and fitness for the particular position. To meet this responsibility school systems use a combination of various administrative practices, including the use of the formal application blank, letters of reference, college credentials, reports from employers, personal interviews, oral and written examinations, health examination, teacher certificates or licenses, observation of classroom work, eligible lists, and probationary teaching.

THE FORMAL APPLICATION BLANK

The use of the formal application blank is a practice generally accepted in all programs of teacher selection.[9] Some systematic method of collecting factual material concerning the candidate's qualifications is necessary; and in order to have such information uniformly listed and arranged for easy reference, superintendents and personnel officers use the formal application blank as a primary step in the selection of teachers.

All the thirty-seven school systems in this study use formal application blanks, each having adopted a general application form or several special forms to fit specifically the particular administrative organization and the rules and regulations of the local board of education. Twenty-seven of these cities use only the one general application form or blank which is adaptable to all teaching and supervising positions in the particular system. The other ten cities use two or more special forms, covering a variety of special fields and subjects, such as: elementary teacher, high school teacher, kindergarten teacher, teacher of trade courses, teacher of commercial subjects, and others.

[8] Criterion VII, p. 16.   [9] Criterion VIII, p. 17.

The application blanks vary considerably in size. One city (Philadelphia) uses a three and one-half by six inch card, both sides to be filled out. Five cities use a single blank, eight and one-half by eleven and three-fourths, to be filled out on one side only. Twenty-one cities use a similar sized single sheet, but require information on both sides. Eleven cities use a folder style of four pages.

It is the practice in all the cities to furnish formal application blanks upon request, although one city does not send out the blank until just before a competitive written examination is scheduled. Only one city, Los Angeles, charges a registration fee. In that city a charge of two dollars per application is made, and applications not accompanied by such remittances are not considered. These fees cannot be refunded after the application has once been filed. One other city, Houston, requires that postage amounting to four cents per name for each reference be enclosed with the application to "cover expense." In another city, New York, the application is held invalid unless an affidavit is duly filled out and sworn to before a notary public. For the most part, applications are kept on file for three or five years. Four cities, however, definitely state that applications are to be renewed at the end of one year; one, at the end of two years; and a third, that applications are to be renewed on request.

A detailed study of the application blanks used in the thirty-seven cities shows great variation in both uniformity of arrangement and the number of items or questions. Nevertheless, the information desired can be classified under the following headings: (1) personal data, (2) educational data, (3) teaching and trade experience, and (4) references. These general classifications are similar to the findings of Davis[10] and Nietz.[11]

Only five of the cities ask for both academic and professional training with names of specific courses studied, while eleven require either a certified statement or transcript of courses and degrees or a state certificate. Eighteen, or nearly one-half, of the number of cities studied request a recent photograph of the applicant. Seven ask for

[10] Davis, Calvin O., "What Qualifications Are Demanded of Teachers?" *Nation's Schools*, 3 : 31–34, January, 1929; 62–68, February, 1929; 71–76, May, 1929; 46–50, June, 1929.

[11] Nietz, John A., "The Current Use of Teachers' Application Blanks." *American School Board Journal*, 76 : 55–56, March, 1928.

the applicant's religious or church affiliation, and one (Birmingham) inquires whether the applicant is engaged in Sunday School work either as pupil or as teacher. One application blank (Louisville) contains a question concerning the magazines read by the applicant, while two (Atlanta and Dallas) ask the applicant to name the educational and professional journals read by him. One city (Oakland) asks for the number of professional books read, and two (Dallas and Houston) ask the applicant to name two or three of the best books on "Education" recently read. Only one city (Detroit) asks for the mental test score of the applicant. The following interesting question is found in the application blank of New York:

> Have you ever been a defendant in a civil or criminal action at law? (Answer "Yes" or "No.") . . . . If "Yes," add such facts as you care to give in a statement to be attached to this application.

The application blank of another city (Portland) contains the following:

> All teachers are expected to take care of roll rooms, make out reports, manage study halls, assist with general discipline, and take an interest in all affairs of the school. Are you qualified and willing to accept these responsibilities? . . . .

While it seems that some items found in these formal application blanks serve little purpose in teacher selection, and while it is quite evident that very important items are lacking in others, yet the formal application can and does have a valuable place in any administrative procedure for the selection of teachers. Undoubtedly it (1) provides a means whereby the selecting agency can obtain necessary information concerning the applicant; (2) enables the selecting agency to have such information concerning every applicant arranged in a uniform manner, readily filed, and easily referred to; and (3) furnishes comparable information for determining the eligibility of applicants. This information, obtained through the application blank, furnishes the primary basis for the determination of eligibility. Each of the school systems has established certain minimum requirements which applicants must meet in order to qualify, and the application blank must be the first step in the selective process. Because of the long-range nature of the application blank, the information desired should include only those factors which are purely objective and readily determined or verified. This information can be classified as follows:

1. Personal data, including name, address, race and citizenship, date and place of birth, and marital status.

2. Specific training in the special field of work for which the applicant has applied.

3. Professional training as represented by specific and general courses in education.

4. General training as represented by all other college and university courses not included under "1" and "2."

5. Experience in teaching, supervision, and administration.

6. Trade or other experience.

7. References as represented by names, official positions, and addresses of persons who are most familiar with the work of the applicant both as student and teacher or employee.

These seven general headings will include the twenty-five items most frequently found on application blanks as reported in the special studies by Almack, [12] Keller,[13] and Brogan,[14] and are highly essential in determining the eligibility of the applicant in terms of the local requirements. They can be adapted to fit any local conditions. Moreover, they can be verified or investigated, and for the most part objectively evaluated in terms of the minimum or desirable requirements for eligibility. Certified statements or transcripts of all academic and professional credits, showing the number of semester hours and grades, should be furnished by the applicant and should accompany the application or be submitted by the college or university upon request. No application should be considered without such certification of training. The verification of experience and testimonials from references given by the applicant are to be secured by those responsible for the selection of teachers. Any other information asked for on the application blank which cannot be verified or is not objective in nature has little value, if any, in determining the

[12] Almack, J. C., "Selection of Teachers." *The American School Board Journal,* November, 1920, pp. 29, 31.
[13] Keller, Frank, "Use of Teachers' Application Blanks." University of Pittsburgh, Master's Thesis, 1928. (Unpublished.)
[14] Brogan, Whit, *op. cit.,* p. 15.

eligibility of the applicant. Even the photograph, requested by eighteen of the cities, has, at best, only an identification value.[15]

Summary and Conclusions

There are three ways of getting information regarding the applicant: (1) from the applicant himself; (2) from the applicant's references; and (3) from other competent referees. Information from the applicant himself is obtained from his application blank, a personal interview, oral or written examinations, and classroom demonstrations. The use of the application blank is the first step in this procedure to get all desirable information concerning the applicant, and its chief purpose is to determine his eligibility. Both practice as found in the thirty-seven cities and the weight of educational authority justify the following recommendations:

1. The use of the formal application blank is an accepted practice in teacher selection.

2. The application blank provides a uniform method whereby the selecting agency can obtain certain definite information concerning every applicant.

3. In view of the long-range nature of the formal application blank, the information should be purely objective.

4. The information desired should be the type that is readily determined or verified.

5. The information desired should be of the type that will determine the eligibility of the applicant in terms of minimum or desirable requirements of the local school system.

6. The wording of the items, the directions to the applicant, and the arrangement of the items should be such that they can be easily understood and readily followed by the applicant and the information easily checked and evaluated by the selecting agency.

These special findings are essential to meet effectively the general criterion that a program of teacher selection will include the use of an application blank.[16] Even though each system adapts such blanks to fit specifically its needs and purposes, the value of the blanks will be determined by their conformity to these findings.

[15] Tiegs, Ernest W., *An Evaluation of Some Techniques of Teacher Selection*, p. 37. 1928.   [16] Criterion VIII, p. 17.

LETTERS OF RECOMMENDATION OR REFERENCE REPORTS

After the formal application has been received and checked to see if it meets the established requirements, every effort should be made to verify and appraise the qualifications of the candidate. Official credentials from various accredited institutions, and reports and recommendations from accredited references submitted by the candidate furnish exceptional opportunities for such verification and appraisal. The use of letters of recommendation and formal reference blanks is considered quite essential in obtaining the information about the candidate, especially when they are secured from those competent persons who are best acquainted with him and his work.[17]

General letters of recommendation personally presented by the person making application are, at best, of questionable value and no longer used in the larger cities. On the other hand, definite information from reliable sources can be and is most helpful in teacher selection. For the most part, the cities represented in this study consider only written and confidential statements from persons who are listed by the candidate himself on his application blank. This type of information is usually secured in two ways. Some systems use a "reference report" form which is sent to those school officials or instructors with whom the candidate has worked. Others use a personal letter written to those individuals named as references. In either case the information is considered strictly confidential and does not pass through the hands of the candidate.

Twenty-six of the cities use a special form or reference blank for information concerning the candidate. Two of these (Detroit and New Orleans) have three different forms, while three cities (Louisville, Houston, and Oakland) use two forms. Wherever more than one form or reference report is used, one will be a "general" form and the others will be used for special types or classifications of teaching positions or for particular information, such as:

Special reports on manual training and home economics teachers.

Trade and commercial education and experience.

Certification of teaching experience in order to fix the salary of the teacher.

[17] Criterion IX, p. 17.

Special information to be secured from registrars and placement offices of colleges and teacher-training institutions.

Of these cities which use a special form, twenty-three have printed blanks, while three are using mimeographed forms. Three of the cities use a type of reference blank which is merely a general request for information as to the probable worth of the individual candidate or for the qualifications both as a person and as one with the necessary academic and professional qualifications for a stated position in the school system. The simplest form of this type of request or general reference is as follows:

Dear Sir:

M .... of .... has applied for a position as teacher of .... in the .... Public Schools, and has given your name as one who knows her personal and professional qualifications for such work.

A brief statement from you concerning this applicant will be greatly appreciated and used only in a professional way.

Very truly yours . . .

(Columbus, Ohio)

Another type of general request is submitted:

Bureau of Appointments
College of Education

Dear Sir:

The person, whose name appears below, has applied for a position in the .... Public Schools. Before the credentials are given serious consideration, we wish to receive word from you as to the probable worth of this individual to our schools.

You may be aware of the fact that we are interested in considering only candidates of outstanding ability; more especially those who are strongly recommended to us by the schools in which they have received training and which have been able to secure a record of subsequent teaching success.

Please forward to this office confidential statement of your recommendation.

Yours very truly,

File:

Applicant:—

Subject:—

PLEASE RETURN THIS LETTER WITH YOUR REPLY

However, twenty-six of the cities use reference forms which list definite items of varying importance concerning traits and qualities of the applicant. In some cases the items are grouped under headings such as:

> Vitality and personality
> Leadership and executive ability
> Personal qualities
> School management
> Social traits
> Teaching ability
> General information
> Professional information
> Professional traits
> Experience
> Classroom

In others the items, following no particular order, are not classified. A study of these numerous items listed on the various reference forms clearly shows no agreement as to the number of traits or qualities, or "points," on which applicants should be checked or rated. One system lists but three items, while another lists as many as fifty-four. A complete check-up is given in Table V.

TABLE V

NUMBER OF ITEMS LISTED ON REFERENCE FORMS
IN TWENTY–SIX CITIES

Number of Items	Number of Cities
Three to five items	2
Six to ten items	5
Eleven to fifteen items	5
Sixteen to twenty items	8
Twenty-one to twenty-five items	2
Twenty-six to thirty items	2
Thirty-three items	1
Fifty-four items	1

The various items listed and the frequency with which they appear on the reference forms used by these twenty-six cities are found in Table VI. Besides these, there were fifty-five other items with a frequency of six or less. It is apparent that there is little agreement with regard to the items that should appear on reference blanks.

Those that are found in use in ten or more cities are probably significant and follow very closely the findings of Davis,[18] Franklin,[19] and Brogan.[20]

TABLE VI

ITEMS USED MOST FREQUENTLY ON REFERENCE FORMS
IN TWENTY-SIX CITIES

Items Used	Number of Cities
Scholarship (including preparation)	26
Teaching experience	26
Success in discipline or managing	19
Character (including moral character)	18
Health	17
Disposition and ability to cooperate	17
Notable deficiencies, faults, defects, objectionable features, idiosyncrasies, or eccentricities which make applicant undesirable as a teacher	14
Skill in instruction (including teaching ability)	13
Loyalty	13
General or personal appearance and manner	13
Willingness to employ the applicant in a school for which you are responsible	12
Success in teaching (including teaching results)	12
Personality	11
Opportunities to form your opinion or judgment of the applicant	11
Professional disposition, attitude, vision, or ideals	11
General estimate or rating	11
Tact	10
Physical defects (if any)	10
Sympathetic relations with pupils and parents	9
Evidence of professional growth	9
Teaching experience under your observation or supervision	9
Culture and refinement	8
Qualifications best suited for teaching what grade or subject	8
Initiative and energy	7
Standing in community	7

It is evident that many of the items listed are so worded that their interpretation and the replies may fail to give adequate or reliable information. Eleven of the cities use special forms provided with blank spaces which are to be filled in as best suits the individual giv-

[18] Davis, Calvin O., *op. cit.*, pp. 31–34.
[19] Franklin, Ray, "What Superintendents Ask Applying Teachers." *American School Board Journal*, 80 : 51 and 142, April, 1930.
[20] Brogan, Whit, *op. cit.*, p. 23.

ing the information. No rating terms or scales or explanations are indicated; only a notation such as: "Kindly state, in the space provided under the respective headings below, your opinion in regard to this applicant." The other fifteen cities, however, use either a four-, five-, or six-point rating scale, and the individual giving the information merely checks in the proper column to indicate the quality of the trait or characteristic listed. Twelve of these fifteen cities use a five-point scale, such as:

a.	b.	c.
(1) Superior	(1) Superior	(1) Of outstanding superiority
(2) Excellent	(2) Strong	(2) Distinctly superior
(3) Good	(3) Average	(3) Above average
(4) Fair	(4) Doubtful	(4) Average
(5) Poor	(5) Weak	(5) Below average

One city (St. Paul) uses a series of four- and three-point scales which are planned to fit more appropriately the individual items listed on the reference forms. Examples of these are:

Scholarship: (1) Superior (2) Good (3) Fair (4) Poor
Spirit of the school: (1) Decidedly good (2) Good (3) Indifferent (4) Rebellious
Daily preparation: (1) Careful (2) Satisfactory (3) Fair (4) Unsatisfactory
Professional attitude: (1) Strong (2) Weak (3) Lacking
Personal appearance: (1) Fine (2) Good (3) Unprepossessing
Appearance of room: (1) Tidy (2) Ordinary (3) Unsatisfactory

One of the largest cities (Detroit) attempts to define some of the terms used on the reference form so that a common understanding of the trait or quality to be rated may be had by all who rate the candidate. For example, the items:

Vitality—physical development, reserve strength, health.
Personality—the impression produced upon others.
Social intelligence—attitude toward, and contact with, life outside of school.
Professional spirit—attitude toward teaching.
Professional leadership—influence on fellow-workers.
Executive ability—efficiency in achievement.
Adaptability—open-minded cooperation.

Symonds urges: "Particular attention must be paid to the definition of the items in rating scale. On this hinges much of the success or failure of ratings in general. One of the most potent factors causing unreliability of ratings is ambiguity in meaning of the items in the scale." [21] One other city (Minneapolis) lists qualities which are rated on a five-point scale where Points 1, 3, and 5 are briefly explained or defined in order to assist one in interpreting the scale. The individual who is rating the candidate places a check mark on the scale at a point which in his judgment best represents the truth. At the same time the rater may also underline the word or words which clearly describe the person. For example:

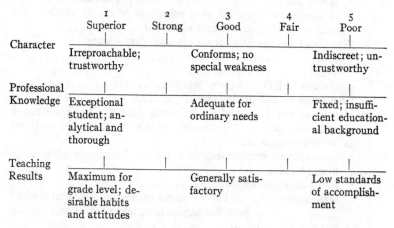

	1 Superior	2 Strong	3 Good	4 Fair	5 Poor
Character	Irreproachable; trustworthy		Conforms; no special weakness		Indiscreet; untrustworthy
Professional Knowledge	Exceptional student; analytical and thorough		Adequate for ordinary needs		Fixed; insufficient educational background
Teaching Results	Maximum for grade level; desirable habits and attitudes		Generally satisfactory		Low standards of accomplishment

Of the eleven systems asking for a "General or final rating or estimate" on the reference blank, only three suggest any method of rating or terms to be used. One city (Kansas City) asks the following:

As compared with teachers you have known of the same general grade, would you rank .... in the HIGHEST 10% ...... NEXT 15% ...... SECOND 25% ...... THIRD 25% ...... FOURTH 25% ......

Another city (Seattle) asks that the applicant be rated in terms of "poor, fair, good, strong, or superior"; while the third (Houston) asks for a general estimate in terms of "poor, fair, average, good, or superior."

---

[21] Symonds, Percival M., *Diagnosing Personality and Conduct*, p. 84. 1931.

In a few cases the letter of recommendation or the reference blank takes the form of a "Report on Teaching Service." While it deals primarily with information concerning teaching experience, this type of report includes many of the items common to the usual reference form. A copy of the most elaborate of such reports is submitted (New York City 1935–36):

Report on Teaching Service

Name of Applicant .... License applied for ....
1. *a.* Applicant's total experience as a regular teacher in your school
   (No. of years)
   ....
   b. Weeks per year .... *c.* Hours per week ....
   d. If service was rendered as a substitute or supply teacher, give total number of days taught each year ....
2. Give the places and dates of such teaching experience:
   ....,.
   ....
   Give name of P.O. address of school ....
   Give subjects and grades taught ....
3. If your answer to any of the following questions is "Yes," please give the essential details on the back of this blank. Has the applicant as far as you know ever
   a. been refused employment as a teacher because of alleged unfitness? ....
   b. failed of reappointment? ....
   c. been made defendant under charges before any school authority? .... *d.* been discharged from any position as a teacher or required to resign? ....
   e. had any controversy with school authorities, with the principal, or with teachers? .... *f.* While under your observation, failed to show industry, integrity, self-command, courtesy, or respect for lawful authority? .... *g.* evidences any PHYSICAL, MENTAL, MORAL or SOCIAL defect, disability or weakness that might interfere with his usefulness as a teacher? .....
   h. failed to show a proper attitude toward AMERICAN ideals and institutions? ....
4. Using the scale: 5—Very Superior; 4—Notably Good; 3—Generally Satisfactory; 2—Somewhat Inadequate; 1—Deficient—state how the applicant should be rated in the following particulars as compared with other regular teachers in your school or district:
   a. Success in instruction ....
   b. Success in discipline ....

    c. Success in clerical or administrative assignments . . . .

    d. Willingness to render extra-curricular service to the school . . . . .

    e. Value of such service . . . .

    NOTE: Specify here or on the reverse side (1) any specially strong points, or (2) any notably weak points in the applicant's service . . . .

5. Check the nature of the work to which the applicant was as a rule assigned:

        Extremely difficult . . . .
        Difficult   . . . .
        Normal   . . . .
        Easy   . . . .
        Very easy   . . . .

6. To what extent can you endorse this applicant for a teaching position in New York City, basing your endorsement SOLELY upon his CHARACTER and PERSONALITY? (Check one)

        Cannot endorse
        Endorse with hesitation
        Endorse moderately
        Endorse with confidence
        Endorse with enthusiasm

7. To what extent can you endorse this applicant SOLELY on the basis of his evidence of EDUCATION and SCHOLARSHIP? (Check One)

        Cannot endorse
        Endorse with hesitation
        Endorse moderately
        Endorse with confidence
        Endorse with enthusiasm

8. *a.* Does the applicant speak English with a foreign accent? . . . .

    b. Is the applicant's habitual speech in any way faulty? . . . .

    If the answer to (*a*) or (*b*) is "YES," please give particulars on the BACK OF THIS SHEET.

9. Would you desire to have the applicant assigned to a school under your supervision? . . . . If not, why not? . . . .

10. Please indicate the basis for your answers to the questions on this blank by a check placed after one or more of the following:

    a. Your personal first-hand knowledge . . . . . .

    b. Official records or reports   . . . . . .

    c. Indirect evidence   . . . . . .

Name . . . .

Position . . . .

Date . . . .

Institution . . . .

Address . . . .

Wherever letters of recommendation or reference blanks are used, the practice is to have them examined by the superintendent, or his authorized agent (either an assistant or a committee of two or more), and used in connection with the personal interviews. Granted that the individuals writing the letters of recommendation or filling out the reference blanks are known or their positions respected, the information is usually studied for two main purposes: (1) To verify teaching experience and general equipment. (2) To ascertain if there are any known weaknesses or undesirable qualities which should require the rejection of the applicant.

One city (Los Angeles) definitely rates the references of all applicants. This rating is done by a committee, called the "Oral Committee," who conducts the personal interviews. The following rating scale is used:

Superior	95–100
Strong	90–94
Average	85–89
Doubtful	less than 85
Weak	less than 80

The percentage mark is indicated on a special form, "Rating on Applicant's References," together with any general remarks, and signed by the chairman of the committee. This rating represents the combined judgment of the several members of the committee and is used in determining the final rating of the applicant.

Many studies have been made of the types of information requested about applicants. In spite of the great variation in qualities or traits listed on the reference blanks, there is a definite tendency on the part of educators and school executives to agree on certain qualities which influence teaching success. As early as 1915, Ballou, in his survey of seventy cities, concluded that the eligibility of candidates should depend largely upon academic education, professional training, teaching experience (quality, not quantity), health, and moral character.[22] Benson, in a somewhat limited study in 1929, listed professional knowledge, general culture, teaching ability, discipline, cooperation, and personal appearance as the most significant qualities

---

[22] Ballou, Frank W., *Appointment of Teachers in Cities*, pp. 130–179.

influencing teaching success.[23] Tubbs, in his survey of practices included in the selection of teachers, found that five factors were most significant in considering applicants: education, experience, health, character, and personality.[24] Furthermore, Brogan, in his comparison of the frequency of occurrence of traits in letters of reference forms used by superintendents and by placement offices, names seven items common to both lists: success as a teacher, personal appearance, scholarship, character, personality, cooperative spirit, and ability as a disciplinarian.[25]

Summary and Conclusions

An analysis of the various items to be found in letters of reference forms in all the thirty-seven cities and a proper classification of such items indicate certain definite factors or qualities which are significant. These are: scholarship, both general and professional; teaching experience; character; success in teaching; success in discipline; cooperation; health; personal appearance; personality; and professional attitude. Since these basic qualities are still accepted as important in determining the suitability of candidates for teaching positions, the information to be sought through the reference form or letter of recommendation should at least be in terms of such specific qualities.

The reference report, at best, will be influenced by three factors: (1) the person giving the information concerning the candidate, (2) the type of blank or form used in recording the information, and (3) the individual or group of individuals who will interpret and rate the information in terms of the requirements of the position for which application has been made.

Accordingly, to make the use of the reference form or letter of recommendation a worth-while procedure in a program of teacher selection, the following suggestions, supported by the weight of practice and educational authorities, are offered:

---

[23] Benson, W. W., "The Selection of Teachers." *Alabama School Journal,* 46 : 7–9, February, 1929.

[24] Tubbs, Eston B., "The Selection of Teachers." *Peabody Journal of Education,* March, 1930, pp. 323–332.

[25] Brogan, Whit, *op. cit.,* p. 30.

1. A printed reference form should be used which is adapted to the needs and purposes of the particular school system.

2. The reference report form should be arranged to include items that call for special information relating to scholarship, both general and professional, teaching ability, professional attitude, character, personality, and health.

3. Different report forms might well be used for at least two different levels of teaching, elementary and secondary, since the classification of teacher traits is best made according to the level of teaching to be done.

4. The reference report should be so worded that all items of information asked for will be clearly understood.

5. The reference report should contain definitions or explanations of the terms used so that all the information received from several sources concerning any one applicant will be fairly comparable.

6. The reference report should be so arranged that the various traits and qualities can be checked or rated in rank-order columns. Best practice clearly indicates a five-point scale.

7. The rating terms used should endeavor to indicate those standards generally recognized in the teaching profession.

8. The reference report should be used for every candidate whose application is being considered.

9. The reference report should be secured from competent school officials and teachers who are acquainted with the applicant and under whom he has taught or studied.

10. The reference report should be used only in a confidential and professional manner.

11. The reference reports of an applicant should be carefully studied by those who are responsible for the interviewing and rating of the applicant.

12. The reference reports should be used in connection with the personal interview with the candidate.

13. The reference reports should be studied to verify the general equipment and teaching experience, and to ascertain if there are any known weaknesses or undesirable qualities or traits which would require the rejection of the candidate.

14. The reference reports should be scored according to a well-

planned rating scale, and form an important part in the final general rating or ranking of the candidate.

15. Wherever possible, at least three reference reports should be secured for each applicant.

16. The final rating of the reference reports should represent the combined judgment of at least three competent examiners or raters.

These specific recommendations are based on the best of the current practices as found in the survey and are in keeping with the trends in modern educational administration. They represent basic detailed steps in the use of reference reports and are essential to meet effectively the criteria that every effort should be made to obtain complete and reliable evidence concerning the qualifications of each candidate; and that every candidate's credentials should include information from competent persons who are best acquainted with him and his work.

CHAPTER V

MEETING THE INDIVIDUAL CANDIDATE

While the various practices thus far considered have been of primary importance, the administrative officers responsible for teacher selection have not been in personal contact with the candidate. All the information obtained has been received through written and documentary sources. It now becomes necessary to arrange to meet the candidate.

THE PERSONAL INTERVIEW

There can be no substitute for the personal interview in a program of teacher selection.[1] Regardless of the information disclosed by the individual's credentials, letters of recommendations, or reference reports, there remain certain personal traits and qualities affecting the teaching efficiency which should be considered. Studies to find scientific measures for evaluating such personal qualities have not provided an effective substitute for this personal interview. It is through the interview that the candidate can be examined with reference to these and to his general fitness. The individual appraisement by the different members of the committee or board of examiners, subjective as it may be, is definitely in relation to the position for which the application has been made and serves to eliminate those who, although they have the necessary training and experience, have not those personal qualifications which the position demands.

Strange as it may seem, of the thirty-seven cities studied, only eighteen definitely state on their application blanks and circulars of information that a personal interview or oral examination is required in the program of teacher selection. While personal interviews with applicants have been, and are, undoubtedly held in many instances in the other nineteen cities, such interviews are at the discretion of the selecting agency, and are not a prescribed requisite for selection or

[1] Criterion X, p. 18.

appointment. One of these cities (Akron) prints in its regulations the following:

> If a personal interview is impossible, it is desirable that you send a recent photograph.

Other examples of regulations governing the discretionary use of the personal interview are given as follows:

> An interview is always desirable; in fact, is frequently required. (Cleveland)

> Personal interview in addition to the written examination is always desirable. (Houston)

> In addition to the written application, a personal application is desired. (St. Paul)

> Persons are rarely appointed without a personal interview. Where practicable, it is best to have an interview with the Superintendent of Schools and with the principal of the school or schools in which the applicant seeks appointment. (Kansas City)

Purpose of the Interview

Where the personal interview is required, its purpose has been definitely stated or its scope outlined so that the applicant might be prepared for this step in the qualifying procedures. An examination of statements found in the rules and regulations of various boards of education reveals that selecting agencies realize the existence of traits and qualities affecting teaching efficiency which cannot be ascertained or measured by a written application or a written examination. To meet this deficiency in the written application and the examination, the personal interview is required. The purpose of the interview is stated in various ways by different boards of education:

> Personal conferences are arranged for the purpose of enabling the Superintendent to judge the applicants as to personality, training, experience, and special fitness for work in school. (Columbus)

> The oral examination aims to ascertain knowledge, education, experience, record as a teacher and student, culture, resourcefulness, and general fitness (personality, etc.) for the position as teacher covered by the license sought. (Washington)

> In this interview the post high school training, teaching experience and

any other experience appropriate to the field of work are appraised. Due note is made of personal characteristics of the applicant, such as appearance, manner, voice, and use of English, including diction and enunciation. Appraisement is also made of the cultural background, as evidenced in the applicant's outside interests, general reading, and recreational activity, and through discussion with the applicant, light is thrown on his ability in constructive thinking, his originality, and his resourcefulness. (Philadelphia)

It is for the purpose of evaluating personal traits that condition the success of a teacher and other qualities of the applicant affecting teaching efficiency which are not evaluated in the written examination and credential rating. (San Francisco)

Oral examinations are given in order to judge the personality of the candidate with reference to the position sought. This examination takes emphatic cognizance of the fact that outstanding qualifications in the form of training and experience may be acquired without the supplementary personal qualities which are as essential to success as an educator. In the oral examination the applicant is examined with reference to personal characteristics, professional ideals, and special fitness for the position sought. (St. Louis)

The examining committee shall regard the oral examination as an opportunity to meet the candidate personally. The personal interview gives the committee an opportunity to meet and judge the candidate as to his general fitness. (Los Angeles)

An Interview Test is given to ascertain the applicant's fitness with respect to personality, mental responsiveness, and use of oral English. (New York)

In a majority of the cities where interviews are held, either the superintendent of schools or the assistant superintendent in charge of the division in which the applicant seeks appointment conducts the interview and rates the applicant. In several cities the practice is to have the principal of the school in which the applicant seeks appointment assist the superintendent's office with the interview. In one city (New York) one member of the Board of Examiners interviews the applicant. In another (Los Angeles) several members of the Examining Committee are asked to interview and rate the applicant. In two cities (St. Louis and Philadelphia) a committee of at least three persons conducts the interview, while in another (Oakland) three members of the Board of Superintendents interview and rate the individual applicant. There is a growing tendency, however, to have the applicant interviewed by individual members of an examining board, named by the superintendent and approved by the board of education. Principals, heads of departments, supervisors, and assistants are asked to serve on these examining committees. As Graves so ably contends, "It is wise for the superintendent (or his assistant) to check upon his own conclusions by having several experienced people interview and rate the same teacher." [2] Symonds emphasizes the same principle when he says: "In general the rating by a single judge is too unreliable to be useful. Single ratings should not be used in the rating of human qualities." [3] Rugg in an earlier study concluded that human character can be treated accurately enough for practical purposes in education only when the rating is the average of three independent ratings.[4]

Conduct of the Interview

In a few of the cities the supervisory officer or a member of a committee of examiners uses a special list or outline of qualities or traits with a score card for recording the results of the interview. In others, only a score card is used to record the interviewer's rating. An examination of all the printed forms used in the various cities reveals many qualities and traits listed. Table VII gives those listed most frequently (page 72).

In their attempts to rate the personal traits and qualities of the applicant, the examiners in the several cities use various methods in their interviews. Informal conversations, oral demonstrations, discussions of professional topics, and questions and answers formed the basis for most of the interviews. In one city (New York) the following procedure was used in the Interview Test:

> The applicant (for a mathematics teaching position) was given a printed paragraph describing a particular method of proof in geometry. He was told to study the paragraph and be prepared to answer the four questions at the end of the sheet. The questions were:
>
> *a.* Interpret the paragraph to the examiner.

[2] Graves, Frank P., *The Administration of American Education,* p. 196.
[3] Symonds, Percival M., *Diagnosing Personality and Conduct,* p. 95.
[4] Rugg, H. O., "Is the Rating of Human Character Practicable?" *Journal of Educational Psychology,* 13 : 30–42, 81–93, 1922.

   b. Describe two other methods of proof used in the schools.

   c. How would you teach "Consecutive Number Problems" in an algebra class?

   d. Prove some particular theorem in geometry you may select.

The applicant was given five minutes to read over the sheet before being called to answer the questions. While the applicant was presenting his four responses, the examiner recorded on a score card his rating of the applicant as regards:

   a. Personality

   b. Appearance

   c. Poise

   d. Apparent knowledge of the subject

   e. Oral presentation

   f. Ability to demonstrate

In another city (Indianapolis) a printed "Personal Interview Blank" with specific questions and spaces for answers is used. Of the

TABLE VII

QUALITIES AND TRAITS LISTED MOST FREQUENTLY BY INTERVIEWERS FOR RATING

Quality or Trait Rated	Number of Cities
Personal appearance	18
Personal manner	18
Professional attitude	18
Use of English, including diction and enunciation	18
Evidence of culture	17
Recreational activities	16
Voice	16
Professional growth	16
Constructive thinking, including originality, resourcefulness, conciseness	10
Dress	10
Physical appearance	10
Attitude toward work	9
Ability to interpret and answer questions	8
Apparent general background	7
Sense of humor	7
Cheerfulness	7
Poise	6
Personal animation	6
Indication of force	6

twenty specific questions asked on this blank, the following are indicative of the nature of the interview:

1. What recent extension or summer school courses have you taken?

2. Why did you select these particular courses?

3. What have your supervisors said were your greatest difficulties?

4. What have your supervisors said was your greatest strength?

5. What difficulties did you encounter in your practice teaching?

6. What strength did you show in your practice teaching?

7. What is your greatest outside interest (extra-curriculum)?

8. What is your "hobby"? That is, what do you enjoy doing in your leisure time?

9. What professional magazines do you read? Subscribe to?

10. What non-professional magazines do you read? Subscribe to?

11. What are your future plans for professional growth?

12. Are you willing to take adverse criticism; to adapt your methods to ours; and to agree to abide by our decision as to your success or failure?

In those cities where the personal interview is a definite part of the procedure in teacher selection, a score card is used. This score card may call for a general rating (as in Los Angeles), for separate ratings on specific items (Philadelphia), or for both the general and separate ratings (Denver). With but few exceptions, a five-point rating plan is used, although different symbols, terms, and percentage values are indicated. The prevailing five-point rating plans or scales are as follows:

	A	B	C	D	E
a.					
b.	1	2	3	4	5
c.	5	4	3	2	1
d.	Excellent	Good	Fair	Poor	Very Poor
e.	Superior	Strong	Good	Fair	Poor
f.	Outstanding	Superior	Above Average	Average	Below Average

The few exceptions to the five-point scale are:

a.	Superior	Good Prospect	Mediocre	Not to be considered

    b.   Superior   Strong   Average   Doubtful-weak
      (95%–100%)   (91%–94%) (85%–90%)   (Below 80%)
    c. Outstanding in   Qualified but   Doubtful or not
        ability and   not outstanding   qualified
        fitness.

One city (Indianapolis) not only asked for separate ratings on specific items, but also used different scales to designate the examiner's impressions concerning the separate items under "Personal Data." For example:

Personal appearance:

Inspiring	Favorable	Indifferent	Unfavorable	Repellent

Command of English:

Excellent	Good	Average	Fair	Very poor

Evidence of humanness:

Very friendly	Cordial	Indifferent	Reticent	Aloof

Apparent quickness of understanding:

Very superior	Learns with ease	Ordinary	Slow to learn	Dull

Apparent knowledge of the work:

Complete	Well informed	Moderate	Meager	Lacking

Health:

Excellent	Good	Fair	Poor

There is no general policy concerning the time when the personal interviews or oral examinations are to be held. In some cities it is a matter of convenience; in others, the oral examination is set for stated time after the written examination. A few of the cities arrange to give the oral examination or personal interview the same day the written examination is held. Others schedule definite days for interviews and so announce them. In one city (Denver) the examining board plans its interviews for the year and submits a printed schedule as follows:

The examining board will hold interviews with applicants for teaching positions in the schools on the following dates:

December	♯	April	♯
January	♯	May	♯
February	♯	June	♯
March	♯	August	♯

Applicants are interviewed from 8:30 to 10:00 A. M.
(♯ = days of the month to be inserted)

Another city (Kansas City) usually sets aside two days during the months of March, April, and May for scheduled interviews. A few of the cities (examples: Baltimore and Columbus) reserve Saturday mornings throughout the year for conferences or interviews with applicants, especially those who live outside the city. In Portland, Oregon, the interview follows the application and may come at any time prior to the month of April. An applicant files his written application with which he includes a recent photograph and such reference material as he may wish to place at the disposal of the superintendent. The next requirement is that he make a personal application to the office of the superintendent where he interviews the assistants to the superintendent, the superintendent, or both. The month of April is devoted by the superintendent and his assistants to the study of the written applications and a careful review of the notes made on each applicant at the time of the personal interview.

In some cities, even where the personal interview is required, it is not required of every applicant. For example, in Pittsburgh the applicant should expect to receive information concerning his application only in case an interview is requested or an appointment is offered. In other words, only those applicants whose information and application blanks indicate that they meet the minimum requirements and whose letters or recommendations are satisfactory are granted a personal interview. This policy is followed even where written examinations are held, although on a different basis. The right to take the interview test or the oral examination will depend upon the applicant's passing the written examination first. For example, in Newark only candidates who obtain an average of not less than 75 per cent in the written examination will be eligible for the oral examination or personal interview. In San Francisco the personal interview is held after the written examination. The number permitted to be interviewed is usually one and one-half the number to be qualified, chosen from those standing highest on the list as determined by averaging the results of the written examination. The time of these interviews is generally during the third week after the written examination.

Rating the Interview

In the question of rating the personal interview (oral examination), cities again differ widely in their practices. Some use the interview definitely as a means to eliminate those applicants who do not possess suitable personal qualifications, regardless of their meeting the desirable educational and experience qualifications. Others consider the personal interview a part of an extensive rating scale consisting of many points or credits distributed among many factors, and each factor rated individually and contributing to a total score. Moreover, the question of rating or evaluating the individual items or qualities and traits that are to be considered during the interview presents a variety of practices. Examples of the different types of rating or evaluating are presented:

The personal interview counts twenty-five points out of a possible one hundred points. (Buffalo)

The required passing average on the interview test is 80 per cent. This test is weighted three out of a total of ten. (Philadelphia)

In the personal interview a five-point rating scale is used and a rating of four on that scale by a majority of those rating any applicant shall in itself disqualify that person for placement on the eligible list. The interview counts a possible 200 points out of a total of 1000 points. (San Francisco)

The oral examination counts 40 credits and the written examination 60 credits. (Washington)

The rating given by the members of the examining committee at the oral interviews is a general one based on the applicant's appearance, manner, attitude toward his work, use of English, and ability to interpret and answer questions. The following scale is used as a basis of rating: superior — 95%–100%; strong — 90%–94%; average — 85%–89%; doubtful and weak (failure)—less than 80%. (Los Angeles)

The applicant is either "superior," "good prospect," "mediocre," or "not to be considered." A place on the rating sheet is provided for the examiner to write in "important factors in final decision." (Indianapolis)

The applicant is rated on five items, the examiner using a five-point scale

—A, B, C, D, and E. A "general rating" is also required. In addition he must answer the following question which appears on the rating sheet:
"Question: Shall this applicant be placed upon the eligible list?
Decision: Yes .... No ...." (Denver)

The interview examination is intended to inquire into the applicant's use of oral English, his personality, his general fitness to teach. "In these matters a high standard is maintained by the Board of Examiners." (New York)

As each member of the examining committee rates the applicant, he asks himself the question—"How does this applicant compare with the outstanding and most successful teachers in the system doing the type of work for which he is applying?" [5] (Oakland)

The personal interview, if carefully and thoughtfully conducted, is generally considered one of the most reliable procedures in teacher selection and is widely practiced.[6]

Tiegs, however, does not feel that the personal interview is very successful in terms of a high reliability since it deals too much with the personal equipment of the applicant, and utilizes the subjective judgments of the examiners rather than objective standards.[7] True, the personal interview or oral examination is not a scientific measure of personality. It does recognize the fact, however, that personality is an important factor to be considered in the selection of teachers. Outstanding qualifications in the form of training may be acquired without the supplementary personal qualifications which are so essential to successful teaching. The writer realizes that researches are being made to bring about truly scientific techniques in evaluating personal qualities, but until such techniques are evolved school administrators and supervisory officers must utilize the personal interview. Even with the use of the most scientifically constructed "personality tests," school administrators will continue to use the personal interview. They realize that a more critical selection of teachers with greater emphasis being placed on personality is highly essential to meet more adequately the demands of public education today. Accordingly, they wish to see the applicant, talk with him, and form judgments in terms

[5] Jacobson, E. W., "How to Get Good Teachers." *School Management*, March, 1932, p. 11.

[6] "Administrative Practices Affecting Classroom Teachers," *op. cit.*, Part I, Vol. 10, p. 26.

[7] Tiegs, Ernest W., *An Evaluation of Some Techniques of Teacher Selection*, p. 79.

of their particular situation. The personal interview, without a doubt, is and will continue to be one of the most valuable procedures in teacher selection.

To be effective, the personal interview must be carefully and skill-fully planned. Steiner[8] suggests four basic principles for the guidance of those who are to conduct such interviews. These principles are expressed as follows:

1. The examiner should be able to keep in mind those traits and qualities which a successful teacher should have in the position for which the applicant is applying. The question he should be asking himself is, "How does this applicant compare with the outstanding and most suc-cessful teachers in the system doing this particular type of work?"

2. The examiner should have before him a carefully prepared list of traits and qualities on which he seeks information, and some type of score card for indicating his rating of the applicant.

3. The examiner should plan his interview so that it can be entirely free from any personal embarrassment on the part of the applicant.

4. The examiner should realize that during the interview the applicant is endeavoring to sell himself or, in other words, to make a good im-pression. Hence, the examiner must not permit himself to be carried away or influenced by the applicant's salesmanship qualities; his im-portant task is to judge the applicant's qualities as a teacher.[9]

Any attempt to establish uniform, acceptable procedure for the measurement of personnel through the interview has to depend upon ratings for its validation. Such ratings, to be of value, will not only demand a preliminary period of observation but also require that the interviewer or rater be thoroughly familiar with the field of inves-tigation. "It should be kept in mind, however, that rating is some-thing in which the rater may improve through practice." [10] As stated by Charters and Waples, "It is obvious that any determination of personal traits is at present dependent upon judgment. There is no other available means of identifying the personal qualities that make for success or failure in teaching. Such judgments are secured by two methods: first, by analysis of the literature wherein the writer's judg-

[8] Steiner, M. A., "The Technic of Interviewing Teachers." *The American School Board Journal*, 76 : 65–66, June, 1928.

[9] *Ibid.*

[10] Symonds, Percival M., *op. cit.*, p. 44.

ments are expressed; and second, by oral interviews with expert judges." [11]

Summary and Conclusions

Considering the fact that eighteen of the cities definitely require the personal interview or oral examination as part of the procedure in teacher selection, and that the practice in the other nineteen cities includes a personal interview if possible or convenient, it is evident that the personal interview plays an important part in the program planned to select teachers. Even where the interview was not possible, several of the superintendents reported that they had asked other educational leaders, such as supervisors and teacher-training instructors, who lived in the community where the applicant taught and whose judgments they respected, to conduct the interview for them and to report accordingly. To make the procedure applicable to every school community and to insure a more effective evaluation of the interview the following conclusions based on accepted practices and administration are presented:

1. The personal interview should be a definite part of the administrative procedure in teacher selection.

2. The personal interview should be planned to evaluate the personal traits and qualities that condition the success of a teacher in the position for which he has applied, and any other characteristics of the applicant affecting teaching efficiency which are not and cannot be evaluated in the credential rating, the written examination, or the classroom demonstration.

3. The personal interview should be so planned that it can be used as a means to eliminate those applicants who do not possess suitable personal qualifications.

4. No person should be called for a personal interview who does not satisfactorily meet the minimum or desirable requirements or qualifications for the position for which application has been made.

5. Not less than three examiners or interviewers should meet each applicant, confer with him, observe his personal traits, and report their findings or ratings.

[11] Charters, W. W. and Waples, D., *The Commonwealth Teacher-Training Study*, p. 51. 1929.

6. Each examiner or interviewer should make an individual report on each applicant interviewed.

7. The examiners or interviewers should be definitely acquainted with the qualities a successful teacher must have in the position for which the candidate is applying.

8. The judgments of each examiner or interviewer should be made definitely in relation to the particular position.

9. A uniform check list or outline of traits and qualities on which information is sought should be used. This list or outline should be the result of careful planning, should fit the type of position and level of teaching for which the applicant is interviewed, and should be subject to change from time to time as changing classroom practices and techniques affect teacher qualifications.

10. A type of score card or rating sheet should be used by each examiner or interviewer. It should provide for separate ratings on specific items and for a general rating or recommendation.

11. A rating scale should be used in connection with the rating sheet. Practice seems to favor a five-point rating scale for this. In any case, the scale should make it possible to indicate the "superior" or "outstanding" and the "good" candidates from those who are to be rated less than "good."

12. There should be common agreement among the interviewers as to the definitions of the items used in the rating scale. If necessary, descriptive explanations should be available in order to avoid any ambiguity in the meaning of the items.

The specific criterion includes more than just a provision for a personal interview, if possible, with every qualified candidate.[12] Every step in the procedure must be planned in terms of good administrative practice and must lead to careful elimination and the best possible selection. These special recommendations include the important steps in that procedure which are in keeping with the general criteria and considered necessary if the personal interview is to be effective.

THE PRACTICAL TEST OR DEMONSTRATION OF TEACHING ABILITY

Another procedure in the program of teacher selection is what is frequently termed the "practical test" or demonstration of teaching

[12] Criterion XI, p. 19.

ability. The applicant is required to present or teach a lesson, or a series of lessons, for the benefit of those with whom the application has been filed, or be visited by accredited supervisory officers who observe the applicant teach his own class. This practical test is not to be confused with a type of demonstration to ascertain the technical knowledge or skill possessed by an applicant, such as a test or examination to ascertain the applicant's skill in the use of certain types of machines, tools, musical instruments, gymnasium apparatus, or in singing, or in speaking a foreign language. The purpose of the "practical test" is to determine the applicant's teaching ability in a classroom situation. It is a personal observation of classroom work and provides the opportunity for selecting agencies to observe and judge the applicant's ability to teach.[13] This procedure is a highly satisfactory one, since an experienced supervisory officer can gain a reliable opinion of the applicant and his work by a visit in the classroom and by observing the extracurricular activities conducted by him. It also makes it possible to judge somewhat the relationship of the applicant to his co-workers and even to the community in which he is teaching.

A detailed study of the practices in the school systems represented reveals that only eleven of them definitely require a "practical test" or demonstration of teaching ability for all applicants. The regulations governing teacher selection in these eleven cities specifically state that the observation of classroom work by some designated supervisory officer is a requirement in computing the final rating of the applicant. It is to be borne in mind, however, that many of the selecting agencies in the thirty-seven largest cities consider a graduate of a standard or certified normal school or teacher-training institution has met this requirement of "observed teaching" by successfully passing the practice-teaching and observation courses required for graduation. In those cities with municipal teacher-training institutions or where the state institutions are closely cooperating with the city systems, satisfactory supervision of practice teaching and close cooperation with the faculties of the institutions and the practice centers can and do meet this requirement. In some cases the possession of a state certificate has been accepted as prima-facie evidence that the applicant has successfully completed a required number of prac-

[13] Criterion XI, p. 19.

tice-teaching hours. Since many of the larger cities require a year or more of teaching experience as a necessary requirement for appointment, especially for secondary school positions, the practice in a majority of them has been to accept in lieu of the practice test the certification or recommendation of the applicant's former and present supervisory officers concerning his teaching ability. Nevertheless, in spite of these previously accepted substitutes for the practice test, and even though regulations governing selection of teachers do not definitely require such test, superintendents and personnel officers in all of the thirty-seven cities plan "wherever possible" to arrange for an observation of the applicant's classroom work.

This requirement of the practical test or teaching demonstration is expressed in different ways. For example, one city (Boston) notifies each applicant that all candidates for permanent day school certificates who receive a mark on the written examination sufficiently high to warrant visitation, are visited in the classroom by a member or representative of the Board of Examiners, and the results of the classroom demonstration are given weight in determining the credit to be allowed for "experience in teaching. In general candidates who are employed in or near the city will be visited in their own schools; other candidates will in general be required to give a teaching demonstration in one of the public schools of the city." In Columbus the applicant is notified that wherever possible arrangements are made for the superintendent to observe the actual teaching work of the applicant for a teaching position. A report of superior teaching based on such observation is considered a very important recommendation. In Buffalo the notification reads, "The candidate must be prepared to demonstrate his ability to teach (*subject*) in accordance with the best modern methods." Another regulation reads:

All applicants for initial day school positions who receive a mark on the written examination sufficiently high to warrant visitation shall be visited in the classroom by a member or representative of the Board of Examiners, and the results of the classroom visitation shall be given due weight under Caption II of the requirements for eligibility. Applicants who are employed in or near the city shall be visited in their own schools; other applicants shall, if possible, be required to give a teaching demonstration in one of the public schools of the city. (Philadelphia)

A few cities require the "practical test" or demonstration only for some positions or for certain classes of applicants. In one case the requirement reads as follows:

> A graduate of an approved college or an approved normal or teacher-training school, other than the State Normal School or the City Teacher-Training School, will be assigned to a practice center and required to do at least 10 hours of supervised teaching.
>
> The examination given applicants for the position of teacher of physical training in junior high schools shall include, in addition to the written examination now provided, a practical test in which the applicant shall demonstrate his personal physical proficiency and his ability to teach a group of pupils either in a gymnasium or on a playground. (Baltimore)

In another city (Philadelphia) one finds that

> In physical and health education the applicants are given the opportunity to demonstrate their teaching ability with a regularly assigned class from the school.

In a third city (New York), for a license as teacher in the high school a practical teaching test of at least one forty-five minute period in a city high school is required by the Board of Examiners. In this teaching demonstration a "satisfactory qualifying rating" is necessary if the candidate is to be considered. The head of the department, the special subject supervisor, or the principal of the school is usually assigned by the Board of Examiners to supervise this period of teaching and to rate the applicant. In the elementary field, certain positions call for the teaching test, in which the applicant is called upon to teach the class an assigned lesson involving elementary practices in the use of woodworking tools and in drawing, homemaking, and industrial subjects. For a license as Special Teacher of Health Education, an applicant is required to demonstrate his ability to teach health education in a lower, a middle, and an upper grade of an elementary school in accordance with the requirements of the city syllabus.

Rating the Demonstration of Teaching Ability

Even where the "practical test" or demonstration is required, it is quite evident that it has different values in the final rating of the applicant. In one city (Baltimore) the average attained in the practice teaching and the average attained in the written examination have equal weight in determining the applicant's standing on the eligible list from which appointments are made in numerical order. In another city (New York), if the applicant fails his teaching test, he will be given as promptly as possible a second opportunity to pass it. If he fails the second test, he will be refused a license; but he may without prejudice enter a future examination which must be taken in all its parts. In a third city (Boston) the teaching demonstration counts a possible 300 points of a 1000-point maximum. Those who fail to obtain a mark of 60 per cent in the teaching demonstration are regarded as failing. Moreover, high grades or rating in the written examination will not offset a failure in the teaching demonstration.

Summary and Conclusions

Certainly one of the best practices to follow in determining the teaching abilities of an applicant is to observe him in a teaching situation.[14] Selecting agencies are recognizing more and more the value of this first-hand information concerning the applicant and, wherever possible, are requiring the practical test or demonstration of teaching in some form in computing the final rating of candidates or in eliminating those whose lack of teaching ability renders them undesirable. The observance of the following principles concerning the practical test will aid materially in a program of teacher selection:

1. Actual demonstration of teaching ability in the classroom should be of first importance in any program of teacher selection.

2. The superintendent, members of the board of examiners, or those delegated the responsibility of teacher selection, should be in close contact, directly or through competent representatives, with the normal schools and teacher-training institutions so that the teaching ability of prospective graduates can be properly determined.

3. Experienced teachers who are applicants for positions should be observed, if possible, in their own teaching situations and their teaching ability rated.

4. If such visitation is impossible, the applicant should be re-

---

[14] Criterion XI, p. 19.

quired to do practice teaching or give a demonstration in the system where she is seeking appointment.

5. No matter what may be the ratings on any written examination or on any educational qualifications, no applicant should be considered for a teaching position who does not show teaching ability which meets the approved standards set by the selecting agency.

MEDICAL OR PHYSICAL EXAMINATIONS

Mindful of the rights of pupils in our public schools, the responsible agencies should select only those successful candidates who are physically normal and who are able to perform efficiently the usual instructional and administrative duties, both curricular and extra-curricular, of a teacher.[15] Moreover, the welfare of the school staff certainly demands that only those who are physically fit should be selected. At the same time, the interests of the taxpayer demand that the teacher be selected who is able to meet those health and physical requirements necessary for effective teaching. Frequent and continued periods of absence or even "forced" attendance of teachers who are physically unfit undoubtedly make for a serious loss in pupil achievement and this adds to the cost of public education. Since in some of our city school systems teachers are eventually placed on permanent tenure and have pension rights, the physical examination should be required and should be so conducted that each candidate selected becomes a thoroughly desirable risk from the health standpoint. As Graves so aptly states, "Assurance of sound physical condition is of importance not only to protect the children's welfare but to guard against undue requests for sick leave and retiring allowance."[16]

An examination of the practices in these thirty-seven cities reveals that twenty-three definitely prescribe "physical fitness" as one of the qualifications for teaching and lay down specific procedures to determine such physical fitness. Fourteen of these twenty-three cities require a physical examination under the direction of the board of education, either through the medical director of the school system, the health department of the city, or the health officer of the district. Ten

[15] Criterion XII, p. 19.
[16] Graves, Frank P., *The Administration of American Education*, p. 199.

cities require health certificates attested by a reputable physician in the presence of a notary; but in practically all of these the attesting physician need not be designated by the board of education. In fact, the physician may live in another city or state, and be unknown to the board of education, the superintendent, or the examining officer. In eight of these ten cities no date is required by rule or regulation to indicate that the examination is recent. It is to be hoped that the value of the health certificate is seriously questioned where the date does not approximate that of the application. One city (Houston), however, definitely requires that the health certificate be dated within ten days of the date of the application. Another city (Boston) requires that the health report "be made out upon the physician's official stationery and state explicitly that it be given on the basis of a physical examination."

The following regulations are typical of those cities which require a physical examination of all applicants:

> Any person appointed teacher or principal must pass a physical examination given by the Medical Director of the Board of Education, who shall certify that the person is in sound physical health. If such a certificate cannot be secured, a contract shall not be issued. (Detroit)

> All candidates for appointment as a teacher or a substitute teacher must undergo a physical examination. (Baltimore)

> Applicants for licenses shall be required to pass satisfactorily a medical examination given by a physician employed by the Board of Education. (New York)

The following regulations are typical of those cities which require a health certificate:

> All applicants must furnish a certificate of good health from a licensed physician. (Minneapolis)

> The applicant is required to answer the following question: Can you furnish a certificate of good health? While the certificate may not be requested, the Board of Education has set up the following regulation: Whenever called upon to do so by the Board of Education, each teacher shall furnish a health certificate or other evidence satisfactory to the Board of Education, showing that the teacher's health is good and that he or she is physically able satisfactorily to perform the duties for which employed. In case a teacher is unable to furnish such evidence, his employment at the Board's discretion may be terminated. (Dallas)

The applicant must file with the Board of Examiners a health certificate signed by a duly licensed physician certifying that the applicant has no physical defect or condition of health that will prevent the rendering of satisfactory service. (Rochester)

Thus, in determining the physical fitness of applicants for teaching positions, cities employ various standards. They may be classified as follows:

1. General statement of health by any licensed physician.

2. General statement of health by a designated physician or health officer.

3. Physical record and examination based on definite standards set up by the Board of Education and conducted by duly appointed health officers or medical examiners.

Under standards 1 and 2, physical fitness is determined by those who, in most cases, may know little or nothing about the demands of the teaching profession upon the teacher's physical condition. There are those who still believe that when an individual cannot do anything else, he can teach. Cripples, those hard of hearing, those with serious deformities of arm and hand, those with impaired vision and even defective speech have been recommended as fit for teaching and duly appointed.

In a few school systems, however, the dangers and the inefficiency of such lax methods have been realized and educators and health officers have joined hands in setting up definite physical standards for the teaching profession. These standards are made available to all applicants; and in a few cases (Baltimore and New York, for example) heads of institutions preparing candidates for teaching positions are sent printed information concerning the physical standards required for teachers and are urgently requested to bring such information to the attention of faculty members and prospective applicants. The physical standards as established by such cities as Denver, Los Angeles, New York, Baltimore, and Oakland, California, are especially to be recommended. Two of these cities, Baltimore and Los Angeles, include in their enumeration of physical standards a list of the defects that may impair the eligibility of any applicant and for which the physician or health officer must make careful examination.

Rating of Medical or Physical Examination

As a result of the physical examination, candidates are grouped or classified in different ways by the several systems. In one city (Chicago) each candidate, as a result of the examination, is placed in one of two groups as follows:

Group (1), which includes those applicants who are physically sound or whose physical imperfections are so slight as to have no prejudicial influence on efficiency in school work. These imperfections, however, if detected, must be set forth fully and completely in the physical examiner's report.

Group (2), which includes those whose physical imperfections may have a prejudicial influence on efficiency in school work.

All candidates falling under (1) are accepted and all falling under (2) are rejected. Should the physical examiner be in doubt as to where the candidate should be placed, he may call for consultation one of the four "consulting physicians" appointed by the Board of Education. The result of this consultation is final.

In another city (San Francisco) four classifications are made on the results of the physical examinations: Class A (excellent; fully serviceable); Class B (passable, but with minor remediable defects); Class C (probably serviceable, but with moderate remediable defects); and Class D (physically unfit for service). Candidates falling in either Class A or Class B are placed on the eligible lists for two or three years. Those in Class C are held in the group eligible for one year only, pending correction of the defects as shown by their being placed in Class A or Class B. Those in Class D are not placed at all.

A third city (Baltimore) sets up three classes or groups based on the results of the physical examinations:

(a) Those found free of physical defects and up to the standard designated by the Board of Education, who are recommended for appointment. (b) Those with remediable defects, who are granted provisional appointments only, pending the satisfactory treatment of existing defects. If during this period of probation, such remediable defects impair in any way the applicant's efficiency as a teacher, permanent appointment is denied. (c) Those with irremediable defects who are rejected.

Where remediable defects are found, several systems provide for re-examination or subsequent examination. In Los Angeles, for example, the physical examination record for such a candidate will contain the following signed statement by the examining physician:

> On account of certain conditions noted above, this applicant will require a subsequent examination before being fully recommended. No evidence of any contagious disease is present. The applicant's condition is such as to warrant being elected as a probationary teacher and tried on duty. Should reappear for subsequent examination about ⎯(date inserted)⎯ .

In Oakland the applicant receives from the office of the superintendent a health examination blank addressed to the Examining Physician, Health Development Department, and authorizing a health examination of the applicant. The applicant is directed to make an appointment with the Department and to present himself for examination at a time set for that purpose. The health examination blank is so arranged that it permits the examining officer to report his findings on the various parts of the examination, and to give his recommendations. If the applicant is not recommended, the blank requires the examining physician to state the reasons for such non-recommendation.

Teacher Training and the Physical Examination

Since many of the physical defects which usually bar candidates have had their beginnings or were discoverable during the high school or normal training period, it is certainly in the interests of efficient school administration to guard against training young men and young women for the teaching profession who will be unable to meet the necessary physical requirements. It is to be regretted that a considerable number of training-school and college students could not have been eliminated because of their physical unfitness before they entered upon their training, or guided into other fields of endeavor. Cities which have training or normal schools should exercise particular care in determining those high school graduates who are permitted to enter such institutions for teaching careers. Happily, many cities are demanding a physician's statement or some type of physical examination of high school graduates as a prerequisite to normal school admittance; and in some instances applicants for admission to teacher-training institutions are required to take a complete physical examination under the direction of the physician in the employ of the institution or the state.[17]

Several of the larger cities have seen the need for such careful selection and have already set up definite physical requirements for entrance into training institutions under their control or with which they are closely affiliated. For example, Baltimore requires that all graduates of its high schools who are eligible for entrance into the normal schools must undergo physical examination prior to their entrance. Those with remediable defects must have them corrected before admission, and those with irremediable defects are notified that they cannot be recommended for admission. New York City, which has practically the same requirements, has the physician's report forwarded to the Physical Standards Committee of the Board of Examiners and these reports are carefully scrutinized before notice of approval is sent to the training school principals. Where there are remediable defects, the applicant has the privilege, through treatment, to remove the disability in time for admission. Where a longer period is necessary to correct the deficiency and where it seems likely that the disability might be ultimately removed, the applicant is recommended for conditional admission. In such cases, however, a definite time is set for the correction of the defect.

In this connection, it seems highly necessary that wise and careful guidance should be given to pupils in our high schools who contemplate following a career of teaching.[18] They should be made acquainted with the physical standards required and those who are physically unfit should be appraised of the fact. It is far better in every way to face the truth in such matters early; and the school which does not have the courage to accept this responsibility is guilty of gross misrepresentation. Even those pupils who seem to have remediable defects will save time and possible disappointment if they are so advised. Proper measures can then be taken toward the removal of such defects before admission to professional study is sought.

---

[17] Graves, Frank P., *op. cit.*, p. 184.
[18] National Survey of the Education of Teachers, Vol. III: *Teacher Education Curricula*, p. 29. 1933.

Summary and Conclusions

The importance of the physical fitness of any teacher makes mandatory a careful check on the physical and health condition of every successful candidate.[19] This naturally becomes a necessary procedure in any program of teacher selection, and to be effective should include provision for the following requirements:

1. A physical or medical examination should be required of every successful candidate for a teaching position.

2. This examination should be a very careful, complete, and thorough one. The board of education, acting through its executive officer and his staff, and with the best medical advice available, should set up the health and physical standards for teachers. These standards should include definite information covering those defects which, in their opinion, will impair the eligibility of candidates for permanent appointment. After these standards have been established, the examinations should be given by competent examiners who are approved by the medical profession.

3. The physical or medical examination should be given with a strictly professional purpose to be thoroughly fair to each candidate. The standards should be made available to every candidate, and occasional publicity should be given to health requirements for teachers—especially in teacher-training institutions.

4. The examining physician should be responsible to the superintendent and required to make his definite recommendations to that officer.

5. The examination should be given in the community where the position for which the candidate is applying exists.

6. As a result of the examination, candidates should be classified into three groups. Group 1 should include those found free of physical defects and meeting the standards established for that community by the board of education. Group 2 should include those with remediable defects which may have prejudicial influence on efficiency in teaching; and Group 3 should include those with irremediable defects.

7. Any candidate assigned to Group 2 by the examiner may be granted provisional assignment or appointment only, pending the

[19] Criterion XII, p. 19.

satisfactory treatment of such existing defects. A definite time should be set for the correction of the defects and a subsequent examination required before assignment or appointment is recommended.

8. Any candidate assigned to Group 3 should be rejected.

9. All teacher-training institutions should require medical examinations before admission. Such examinations should be in keeping with those health and physical requirements necessary for teaching.

10. The guidance program in high school and teacher-training institutions should include definite instruction in the health and physical standards of the teaching profession.

These recommendations are necessary to meet effectively the underlying principle that the certification of health and physical fitness be a required qualification in every program of teacher selection. Moreover, they help to promote at various levels in the preparation and selection of teachers those standards which will guarantee, as far as possible, candidates who can meet health and physical requirements necessary for effective teaching. Considerable practice and the weight of educational authorities approve these recommendations.

CHAPTER VI

USING THE WRITTEN EXAMINATION

PRACTICE IN THE LARGER CITIES

ALTHOUGH the use of written examinations as a procedure in teacher selection is very limited and need not be a necessary part of the program,[1] the written examination is required in eleven of the thirty-seven cities studied. In these eleven cities written examinations are required for all teaching positions. In three other cities written examinations are required for positions only in certain stated divisions of the system. For example, one requires the written examination for teaching positions in kindergarten, primary, and intermediate grades, and in the junior high school; but for senior high school teaching positions the regulations read:

> Fitness for appointment to teacher in Senior High Schools shall be determined by careful scrutiny of such diplomas and certificates of graduation as may be issued by colleges of good repute or by examinations oral or written disclosing qualifications in the subject or subjects which the candidate proposes to teach. Candidates who cannot show these qualifications cannot be considered. Proof of success in the actual work of teaching, as well as the possession of the requisite knowledge, will be considered. (Baltimore)

In another city (St. Louis) the following regulation applies:

> Written examinations are held regularly for applicants seeking positions for which no special collegiate training is given in the standard colleges and universities or teacher-training institutions, such as the positions of school nurse, attendance officers, stenographers and clerks.

Two other cities have provisions which make written examinations optional with the superintendent. For example, in Denver

> Examinations, either written or oral, are held from time to time by a committee appointed by the superintendent for the purpose of placing names on the eligible list.

[1] Criterion XIII, p. 20.

93

and, again, in Kansas City

> Certificates to teach in the Public Schools may be obtained by either of the two following methods: First, by presentation of satisfactory transcripts of academic and professional courses taken in preparation for teaching, and passing such oral and written examinations as may be required. Second by passing a complete oral and written examination on academic and professional subjects.

The other twenty-one cities in the study do not set up written examinations as a requirement or use them in their established program for teacher selection. For the most part, (1) possession of a teaching certificate issued by the State Department of Education, (2) evidence of having met the minimum requirements or qualifications, or (3) an evaluation of references, scholastic records, and other credentials is deemed sufficient. The following statements from official information to applicants clearly illustrate this practice:

> We do not undertake teachers' examinations but fill all places on information received through applications and credentials. (St. Paul)

> Examinations, other than the physical examination, are not given in the selection of teachers. (Oakland, Calif.)

> The Superintendent of Schools shall keep a register of all applicants for employment in the schools and shall devise methods of rating the applicants by training, experience, and personal qualifications. He may discard from this register after a reasonable time all applications of those whose rating is so low that there is no likelihood of their employment. (Indianapolis)

PURPOSE OF THE WRITTEN EXAMINATION

In those cities where written examinations are required or are sometimes used at the discretion of the superintendent and his staff, it is evident that such examinations are held for four major purposes. These are: (1) To test the applicant's proficiency. (2) To establish eligible lists. (3) To make it possible to list eligibles on the basis of averages obtained in competition with other applicants. (4) To establish a basis for the issuance of teacher licenses or certificates. Various boards of education have expressed these purposes in their official notices and regulations:

> Under the provisions of the State Education Law and the rules and regu-

lations of the Board of Education, all appointments to a teaching position must be made from an eligible list determined by examination. (Buffalo)

In the preparation of these graded lists (eligible lists) the Superintendent of Public Instruction and his Assistant shall ascertain by competitive examination the relative qualifications of those candidates who desire appointment and place the names of the accepted candidates upon said graded lists in the order of their respective qualifications so ascertained by such competitive examination. (Baltimore)

To test the applicant's proficiency in the subject or departmental subject for which he or she is an applicant. (Jersey City)

Such eligible lists shall be prepared by the Division of Examinations under the direction of the Superintendent of Schools, on the basis of information received from the principal of the Normal School, or the results of examinations conducted by the said division, and of such other data as may be secured by the Superintendent of Schools. (Philadelphia)

The relative merits of applicants and their respective ratings shall be determined in part by the results of a written examination. (Los Angeles)

The written examination for teachers shall be designed to discover the intelligence of the teacher, his ability to comprehend and discuss educational problems and situations, and his attitude toward his work. It shall not be concerned primarily with subjects of instructions. (Los Angeles)

The Board of Examiners annually conducts examination of candidates who desire to qualify as members of the supervisory staff and as teachers in the day and evening school service. The examinations given as aforesaid shall be designed to test the training, knowledge, aptness for teaching, and character of the candidates. (Boston)

All candidates for positions in the educational department, except graduates of the Normal School who have passed an entrance requirement examination and have received elementary certificates, shall be required to pass an examination conducted with reference to the positions for which they are candidates, and from which spectators, except members of the Board of Education, shall be excluded. No member of the teaching force may be employed without a certificate from the Board of Education, and no certificate shall be issued without an examination. (Chicago)

SCOPE OF THE WRITTEN EXAMINATION

The written examinations, where used, have always included examinations in professional subjects, such as "Special Methods," "Theory and Practice," "Psychology," and the like. Nine of the cities, in addition, require written examinations in subject matter covering a range of subjects represented in the various divisions and departments of the school systems and for which vacancies exist or are likely to exist in the near future. It is to be kept in mind that even though the applicants have filed certified records of college preparation and specialization in their major fields, and have met the educational requirements established by the local system, they must take the written examinations in the special subject matter, majors and minors often being required. In one system, however, where a written examination is required in "subject matter of collegiate grade in two departments to be selected," an option is provided as follows:

> Certificates and diplomas from standard institutions will be accepted in whole or partial fulfillment. A candidate who presents certificates or diplomas showing satisfactory completion of two college courses, each covering at least three semester hours, or the equivalent, in a subject, need not take the examination in that subject. (Baltimore)

The same system provides an option in the case of some of the examinations in "Theory" and "Methods": "Candidates may submit certificates or other credentials of standard institutions in whole or partial fulfillment of the examination, provided they have had five or more years of approved experience in teaching." Recently the city of Newark announced that candidates may be exempted from the written examination in "Principles of Secondary Education" if this subject is covered by college diplomas or by certificates from approved institutions.

A list of the professional subjects in which candidates were examined in the various cities during the past three years, as part of the written examination, includes approximately two hundred different titles. Table VIII lists the twenty subjects appearing most frequently on scheduled examinations.

Where examinations are given in specific subject matter, the number of separate examinations possible is determined by the number of separate subject teaching positions or departments in the particular school system. Recently in one city the list of such examinations included as many as fifty-four, from "algebra" to "vocational guidance." Another city sent out announcements of written examinations which read: "Written examinations will be given for the following

TABLE VIII

PROFESSIONAL SUBJECTS IN WHICH WRITTEN EXAMINATIONS
WERE MOST FREQUENTLY HELD

Title of Professional Subject
Principles of Elementary Education
Principles of Secondary Education
Educational Measurements
Class Management and Methods
Teaching Devices
Child Study
School Hygiene
Educational Sociology
General Theory of the Junior High School
Professional Literature
Tests and Measurements
Professional Information
Theory of Teaching
Educational Psychology
Classroom Procedures
History of Education
School Management
Methods of Teaching (various subjects)
Principles of Education
Theory and Practice (at various levels of education)

types of positions. (The subject examination will include questions in method as well as in subject matter.)" Then followed a list of fifty-three different subjects. Another example of the multiplicity of subject matter examinations is found in a recent announcement of an examination for "Vocational Teacher of Shop Practice," open to men only, issued by the board of education of one of the largest cities. The scope of the examination included both a professional examination and a subject matter examination. Although this examination represented only one department (vocational) in the school organization, candidates were permitted to qualify to teach one only of forty-four different trade subjects, from "aircraft construction and repair" to "woodworking mill practice." For each of these forty-four vocational teaching positions the examination included the following parts:

a. English—the rating in this subject to be based upon all the written work submitted and upon the candidate's command of English as indicated in his oral interview.

b. Theory and Practice of Industrial Education.

c. Trade Analysis—the division of the candidate's trade into its main branches and the separation of these divisions into the fundamental elements required for the preparation of a course in that trade.

d. Methods of Teaching Shop Practice

e. Shop Sketching—freehand representation as required for purposes of illustration in the practice of the candidate's trade.

f. Shop Mathematics—all problems which naturally arise in the practice of the candidate's trade, including the usual shop methods of solution and mathematical principles involved.

g. Shop Practice

Included in this examination was a practical demonstration of technical knowledge and mechanical skill in the candidate's trade.

NUMBER OF WRITTEN EXAMINATIONS REQUIRED OF A CANDIDATE

The number of written examinations required of a candidate for a single teaching position varies from one to six, depending upon the individual school system and, in some cases, upon the type of teaching position for which the individual is applying. In one city (Los Angeles) an essay type examination covering but one topic or problem will meet the requirement, as indicated in the circular to applicants:

> A list of topics shall be submitted from which the applicant may choose a subject for a thesis and these topics shall touch upon the theory and practice of education, methods of instruction, special aims and methods of teaching the different subjects, classroom management, school hygiene, educational psychology, the history and philosophy of education, and the relation of the school to other social institutions and to life.

In a second city (Baltimore) an applicant for a junior high school position may be called upon to write six different examinations. A third city (New York) has a written examination given in two parts, covering subject matter and methods of teaching the candidate's specialty. Part I of this examination is made up entirely of the short-answer type of questions, generally two hundred such questions on the examination paper for elementary school positions and about forty such questions for other types and grades of teaching. Part II is the essay and problem type examination. Part I of the examination is graded or rated first and those who fail to secure a passing grade do not have Part II of their written examination graded. Thus, in actual practice, Part I of the written examination becomes a "selective" or an "eliminating" quiz. Several cities (Boston, Pittsburgh, and Chicago) require written examinations consisting of one major subject and two or more minor subjects. In one of these three cities (Chicago) "Professional Study" is a required minor as is also "English" except in the English group. "Theory of the Junior High School" is a required minor for all junior high examinations. Another city (Washington) stipulates that the written examination cover in general the specific subject matter and the principles underlying instruction and activities in the major subject and its designated minor subjects. A somewhat different type of examination is found in San Francisco, where three examinations are required: "English Usage," "School and Classroom Procedures," and "The World Today." This last examination is designed to test the candidate's acquaintance with the main field of human endeavors of the present day. To this examination there are added a number of so-called optional questions which are so designed that persons of varied interests may compete on an equality.

TYPES OF QUESTIONS USED IN WRITTEN EXAMINATIONS

The written examinations given in the different cities represent all types. One finds the essay type, the short-answer type, the true-false type, the multiple-choice type, the problem type, and a combination type. For the most part, however, use is made of both the essay type and the objective types. In several cities the objective type of examination is given as a separate unit or part of the entire written examination. This practice applies to both the professional examination and the subject matter examination.

TECHNICAL EXAMINATIONS

These same cities which require the written examinations also require some form of what may be termed "technical examination" where the candidates desire to teach certain special subjects. This form of examination, frequently but not always given at the time of the written examination, is designed to have the candidate give a practical demonstration of his special knowledge and skill aside from a teaching situation. Such special subjects include certain commercial subjects (typewriting and stenography), arts and crafts, physical education, home economics, industrial arts, mechanical and architectural drafting, modern languages, music, etc. The nature of the technical examination varies with the subject. In music the candidate may be required to demonstrate his: (*a*) Vocal ability. (*b*) Expertness in playing an instrument of the symphonic group. (*c*) Ability to name title and composer of selections played for him. (*d*) Sight-reading ability. (*e*) Expertness in playing an orchestral piano accompaniment at sight. In shop subjects it might be a demonstration in the use of tools and the candidate's ability to use a working drawing and construct a finished object. In commercial subjects it is generally a demonstration of the ability to write at least eighty words a minute on what is termed average matter and to transcribe the notes on the typewriter. In physical education the requirement may be the ability to do apparatus work, or skill and ability in athletics and dancing; while in modern languages it usually includes the ability to carry on a conversation in the particular language and the ability to read short extracts in the language, the context being given in English. These technical examinations are usually taken before committees from the supervisory and teaching staffs of the special department concerned. Several cities, however, arrange to have this type of examination taken before only one examiner.

SPECIAL REQUIREMENTS IN ENGLISH, SPEECH, AND HANDWRITING

A few of the larger cities have set up special requirements in English, speech, and handwriting as part of the examination of candidates. Several examples of these requirements are submitted:

> A satisfactory standard in written English is required of all applicants. Papers are rated separately on content and on use of English. License will be refused any person whose rating on written English is unsatisfactory, and no appeal from such rating will be entertained. (New York)

The examination paper for a high school license contained the following "note heading":

No examination paper is passable unless it meets the minimum standard required both for content and for language. Answer papers are rated twice; first for content; second, for written English, including sentence structure, grammar, spelling, idiomatic usage, diction, punctuation and capitalization. Candidates are therefore apprized of the importance of reviewing their written English in the time allowed for this purpose. Answers should be phrased in full-sentenced continuous discourse, unless an outline is specifically called for.

San Francisco sets up a definite requirement in English usage in its written examination, which counts one-third of the entire examination and is designed as a test on what constitutes good idiomatic English in its written and spoken forms. Buffalo makes the requirement:

> Candidates must be able to write legibly, spell correctly, and show superior ability in the use of the English language. Since every teacher should be a teacher of English, faulty use of the English language will be sufficient cause for disqualification of the candidate.

In Chicago, in every group of written examinations except the English group, English has been a required minor. Moreover, wherever personal interviews or oral examinations form part of the requirements, the candidate is rated on his use of English, including diction and enunciation. A special "Speech Test" is included in the interview test in New York City. This test usually consists of the reading of a printed paragraph and a list of words by the candidate to the examiner. The examiner stands about the distance of the length of a classroom from the candidate and judges the latter's enunciation and normal speech habits. This test, designed to weed out those who have decided foreign accents and noticeable speech defects, is based on the following standards:

Voice—
  a. pleasant, resonant, poised, authoritative without being harsh.
  b. cultured; native intonation.
  c. loud enough to be heard easily in classroom.
  d. nasality, harshness, aridity, monotony; tenseness should be a bar.

Speech—
  a. should serve as model to young children.
  b. should be distinct enough to be understood with ease, in both private and public speech.

    c. marked lisp or other defect, foreignisms or vulgarisms should be a bar.

Type of Examination—

    a. suitable reading test for habitual voice and speech patterns.

    b. free speech for fluency, diction, intonation, pronunciation.

    c. pronunciation lists.

Two cities require a handwriting test. Since January, 1931, New York City has used a short penmanship test, as it is termed, as part of the written examination for a teaching license. The standard of penmanship demanded is such as to insure a model in handwriting consonant with the demand of the penmanship syllabus of that school system. One such examination paper required each candidate to write the sentence, "William Howard Taft was Chief Justice," in accordance with the following instructions: "In your best penmanship, and in accordance with the standard letter forms set forth in the 'Course of Study and Syllabus in Penmanship,' continue writing the sentence till the time limit (three minutes) is up. Use a new line for each sentence. You should write at least six sentences in the three minutes." Buffalo sets forth the following in its qualifications for teachers in the elementary grades: "Ability to write clearly and legibly on the blackboard will be required of all candidates taking this examination. A test in penmanship will be given to all the candidates except those who present a 'Palmer Certificate.' "

SUMMARY AND CONCLUSIONS

The written examination as a definite procedure in teacher selection is used by less than 40 per cent of the cities in this study; and these cities, for the most part, are the largest in terms of population. The reasons given for this practice in these cities are:

    a. The necessity for a "political-proof" merit basis for teacher selection.

    b. The size of the school system and the number of vacancies to be filled each year.

    c. The very large number of applications each year.

    d. The complexity of the system and its variety of teaching positions, each requiring special qualifications.

    e. The lack of uniformity in standards, course requirements, graduation requirements, and certification requirements on the part of teacher-training institutions and certifying agencies.

Conditions in the smaller cities which use the written examination and practice in the larger cities which do not require the written examination will add little weight to these reasons. Moreover, there are no studies to show that the teachers selected in those cities which do not require the written examination are less well prepared or less efficient than those selected through the medium of the written examination. Moreover, the time, effort, and cost involved in the program of written examinations have not, according to available studies or acceptable information, been justified by the superiority of the teaching staff or the educational product achieved through their use. Certainly, after a study of the facts as brought out in this survey, there is every reason to believe that at least a considerable modification could be made in the use of the written examination as a procedure in teacher selection. Accordingly, the following conclusions are drawn and recommendations made:

1. Written examinations are not necessary to establish a basis for the issuance of teacher licenses and certificates.

2. Eligible lists can be established without written examinations.

3. If written examinations are to be given, they could well be confined to applicants seeking positions for which no special training is given in standard colleges and universities. Subject matter examinations would then be limited and definitely related to such positions.

4. The applicant's proficiency in his major and minor fields of specialization can be readily measured by a careful examination and interpretation of his post-high-school education and training as measured by the extent of such training in standard colleges and universities, and by the scholastic achievements in the various courses. One may well realize the fact that traditional marks with respect to any subject or course studied are unreliable measures; but so are the marks made on a single examination which are conditioned by many factors. However, the average of many such marks over a period of four or five years, in a planned group or combination of courses, has been found to have considerable significance.

5. The written examination does not test the teaching qualities of the applicant.

6. If a graded eligible list should require a written examination, the examination could well be confined to a type which would give excellent professional review. "Among the types of objective evidence there can be none more important than the intelligent use of professional tests. The professional test for teachers cannot yield all the types of information concerning her, but other things being equal, the teacher who knows most about the theory and practice in education will be the best teacher." [2]

7. There would be less need for the written examination of approved certifying agencies and teacher-training institutions would certify and recommend their students who have met the accepted standards of preparation to teach only the position for which they are definitely and specifically prepared and trained.

8. There would be less need for the written examination if the various institutions throughout the country which have been approved for the education and training of teachers would join with the school superintendents and boards of education in developing and enforcing a more professional program for the selection and admission of students for teacher training.

9. The technical examination or practical demonstration of special knowledge and personal skill might still find some place in the program of teacher selection. However, the necessity for this type of examination is gradually growing less and less as special schools and colleges are preparing students for such special work and certifying them on the basis of actual performance ability and skill. Moreover, the practice-teaching experience and the demonstration lesson can well serve to include the technical examination.

10. The special examinations in English, speech, or handwriting should not be required if there is careful investigation and evaluation of the candidate's training credentials. Certainly no teacher-training institution should graduate, recommend, or certify for a teaching position one who is deficient in English or speech or handwriting. Such institutions can easily ascertain the standards required in the teaching profession, prepare their students accordingly, and so certify or recommend them.

11. A better understanding and cooperation between teacher-

[2] Tiegs, Ernest W., *Tests and Measurements for Teachers*, p. 218. 1931.

training institutions and teacher-selecting agencies and a better evaluation of the academic and professional records of candidates will gradually eliminate the written examination. "The tendency is clearly in the direction of minimizing the importance of written and oral examinations, given either by the local authority or by the state, and of increasing the recognition given to evidence of academic and professional preparation made in recognized professional institutions of learning." [3]

RATING OF EXAMINATIONS

While the various city systems have different scales for rating or grading examinations, the procedure followed is fairly uniform and aimed to insure anonymity. A number system is used by which the identity of the examination papers is not known to those grading the papers. This phase of the work is supervised by clerks or assigned executives who have no part in the reading and the evaluation of the examination papers. The assignments of the examiners or marking committees are so arranged that usually at least two examiners will evaluate each question or each paper. The computations are checked again at least once by special clerks or assigned specialists independent of those who graded the papers. Generally those papers which received a grade slightly below but within a reasonable range of the required passing mark are returned to the chairman of the marking committee or, as in several cities, to one so designated for a review and a possible re-evaluation.

Various systems of scoring and weighting the different forms or parts of the written examinations are to be found. In some cases actual scores or ratings are given not only to the written examinations but to other procedures in teacher selection, such as: the oral examination, teaching demonstration, and credentials covering education and teaching. Again, one finds a system where each part of the complete procedure in teacher selection is independently rated and failure on any part will automatically disqualify the applicant; as well as a system where the total of all examinations, records, and

[3] National Education Association, Department of Superintendence, *Twelfth Yearbook: Critical Problems in School Administration*, p. 124. 1934.

credentials are evaluated on a summary basis of 1000 points. Several of these systems are briefly explained below.

In one city (Baltimore) the average attained in a written examination with a value of 100 points and the average attained in practical teaching with a value of 100 points have equal weight in determining standing on the eligible list. The sum of these two averages, divided by two, is the average entered on the eligible list after the name of each candidate for appointment in the elementary grades. In the case of junior high school examinations, each examination must be passed with a mark of 75 per cent.

Another city (Boston) evaluates all the examinations on the basis of 1000 points. The major examination is given a value of 300 points, of which 75 points are allowed for the oral examination in the case of candidates who major in a modern language; 50 points in the case of candidates who major in English; or 75 points for a laboratory exercise in the case of candidates who major in physics, chemistry, or biology. Candidates are required to secure a grade of 70 per cent in the major examination; and language candidates who fail to secure 70 per cent in the oral examination are regarded as failing the major examination, no matter what grade they may receive for the written part of the examination. Each of the two minor examinations has a value of 150 points. Candidates must receive a grade of 70 per cent in the total of the three written examinations. Thus it is possible to secure a very high grade in the major examination and comparatively low grades in one or both minor examinations and still secure a passing grade in the total. Total grades less than 70 per cent of the 600 points are regarded as failures. The remaining credit of 400 points includes a possible grade of 300 points for a teaching demonstration. Those candidates who fail to obtain a grade of 60 per cent in the teaching demonstration are regarded as failing. High grades in the written examination will not offset a failure in this part of the whole examination of the candidate. Candidates who submit evidence of only the required amount of education and experience, with satisfactory credentials, are given a credit of 70 points for what is termed a "satisfactory minimum." Further credit up to 10 points is allowed for educational qualifications in excess of the minimum requirements. In addition, an extra credit up to 10 points for additional teaching experience and a similar credit for "superior evidence of teaching ability" are allowed. These bring the maximum total of points to 1000, and the candidate's final rating is established on this basis. This rating determines his place on the eligible lists.

In a third city (New York) one finds a completely different method of rating. Part I of the written examination is rated on a basis of 100 per cent. The passing mark, however, is never determined in advance, since the examination is deemed purely competitive and dependent upon (1) the number of teachers needed at the time; (2) the difficulty of the examination; and (3) the number of applicants taking the examination. One such examination recently contained the following statement:

> The answers to Part II of the examination will not be rated in the cases of those candidates who do not attain on Part I *a pass mark to be later determined.*

By this method the Board of Examiners can and does arbitrarily eliminate a certain percentage in each examination by raising or lowering the passing mark to suit conditions. In one of its reports, the Board of Examiners commented as follows:

> Owing to the danger of clogging the License No. I Elementary List to the point where a list might outlast its statutory three year life, the Board of Examiners has been forced, as far as possible, to limit the number of licenses to approximately 1500 per year. Consequently, only 828 out of 3330 candidates were licensed as a result of the June examinations and 854 out of the 2921 as a result of the January examinations.

The Board of Examiners chooses approximately the upper 50 per cent of the candidates on Part I of the examination for License No. I. In the case of high school licenses, the passing mark fluctuates from year to year and from subject to subject. For more than ten years the number of persons applying for license in mathematics has been very small and the number actually passing the examination insufficient. At one time in order to provide even a short eligible list for this license, it was necessary to drop the pass mark to 45 per cent. Part II papers, for those who have come within the "agreed-upon" pass mark for Part I, are graded on the same basis. There can be no predetermined pass mark which the candidate must make. Thus the passing mark for a place on the eligible lists will vary considerably.

The lowest passing ratings on several eligible lists published at one time by the Board of Examiners were as follows:

Teacher of Physics	71.41
Teacher of Music	63.23
Teacher of Biology	65.41
Teacher of Freehand Drawing	60.91
Teacher of History (Women)	80.63
Teacher of History (Men)	62.19
Teacher of Homemaking	72.58
Teacher of General Science	62.08

After Part II of the examination has been rated, it is again "independently" read for the quality of its English, and errors are penalized by "demerits" weighted according to the degree of the gravity of the error. A *certain* permissible number of "average demerits" per page has been fixed for each grade and kind of license. The license is refused if the rating on written English is unsatisfactory, and *no appeal from such rating will be entertained by the Board of Examiners*. Those who pass Part II and the written English examination are notified to take the oral or interview test. Only those who make a passing mark on the oral or interview test are notified to take the physical examination. Thus each step in the entire examination procedure becomes a separate examination which selects those who are judged competent to take the next examination or the next step in the examination program. Eligible lists are prepared from the total number of those successfully meeting all the various tests. Under this plan of teacher selection months elapse between the time of the first examination and the placement on the eligible list. On the printed circular of information sent to applicants it is stated that eligible lists resulting from an examination in any subject may be expected approximately from five to seven months after the date on which the written examination was held. In practice, however, it is sometimes much longer. For example, announcements were made late in December of one year concerning the granting of licenses and the creation of the eligible lists of the 116 candidates who took the written examination in November of the preceding year. Also, candidates taking the examinations in the spring of 1935 were not placed on an eligible list until November, 1936.

Another city (Buffalo) sets up the following basis upon which a candidate is rated:

Subject matter examination	40 credits
Professional examination	35 credits
Personal interview	25 credits

A minimum of 75 credits constitutes a passing mark, provided the candidate has secured at least 60 per cent of the total number of credits obtainable in each of the three examinations listed.

A somewhat different basis is followed in the city of Newark, New Jersey. Candidates must obtain an average of not less than 75 per cent (with a minimum of 70 per cent in each part) in the written examination to be eligible for the oral examination or personal interview. In the final rating, the complete written examination counts 50 per cent and the personal interview 50 per cent. A minimum of 37½ per cent is required in both the written and the oral examinations.

In the city of Los Angeles the following scale is used as a basis for the rating of all written examination papers:

Superior	95–100 per cent
Strong	90–94 per cent
Average	85–89 per cent
Doubtful and Weak (Failure)	Less than 80 per cent

Readers of examinations are instructed to give no rating between 80 and 85 per cent; that failures must be rated lower than 80 per cent. It is interesting to note the following instructions issued by the superintendent to the readers of the examination papers:

> In rating papers consideration should be given to the presumable ability of the applicant to write an excellent or just an average, or even mediocre paper. In other words: the same basis should not be employed in rating the papers of an applicant for shop work whose training has been mostly vocational but whose education has been limited, and an applicant to teach English, history, etc., and who should be a college graduate. A school nurse should not be expected to write a paper equal to that of a physician.

In one city where written examinations in both major and minor subjects are required (Chicago), the rating differs with the type of teaching certificate desired by the candidate. All candidates for what is termed the general certificate must attain a general average of 80 per cent with a minimum of 50 per cent in any one subject, provided the major subject shall be counted double the value of any minor paper in the examination. However, candidates for certificates of teacher in elementary school must attain a general average of 75 per cent with no subject below 50 per cent. For certificates of teachers in kindergartens the candidates must be examined in one major and three minor subjects, the major counting 50 per cent and the minors each 16 2/3 per cent. On the examinations they must attain a general average of 75 per cent with a minimum of 50 per cent in any one subject. In all examinations where a practical or oral test is included in the major, the candidate must obtain a mark of 75 per cent or more on the practical or oral part.

In Washington the candidate must make an average of 75 per cent or over in any examination except the physical examination where the passing grade is determined by the medical authorities. The written and professional (or practical) examination counts 60 credits and the oral examination 40 credits.

In Pittsburgh the written examination counts 40 points and the evaluation of official records, teaching experience, and observed teaching counts 60 points. Thus the eligibility of the applicant is determined on a 100-point basis. In this case, however, the written examination is used to eliminate applicants, since only those who receive a mark on these examinations sufficiently high to warrant visitation are visited in a teaching situation by a member or representative of the Board of Examiners.

In Philadelphia the examination for applicants outside the service, usually consisting of a written paper, a demonstration of skill or "technical examination," and an oral examination, has a total rating of 10, with the oral examination counting 3. The relative weights assigned to the elements of any one examination vary in the different types of examinations.

The Teachers' Competitive Examination in San Francisco, in its entirety, consists of three "sections": (1) the written examination consisting of four separate papers, (2) the credential rating, and (3) an oral examination. The number permitted to take the oral examination is usually 1½ times the number to be qualified, chosen from those standing highest on the list as determined by averaging the results of Sections 1 and 2 of the examinations. The number to be qualified on the final eligible lists is determined by need and is taken in sequence from those standing highest on the list in general average standing. This general average is obtained by rating the sections as follows:

Section 1	40 per cent
Section 2	40 per cent
Section 3	20 per cent

No applicant can be qualified who fails to make a grade of 50 per cent or over in any one of the three sections.

In Providence the School Committee rates its teachers on the basis of a 1000-point scale. Five hundred points are on ratings of training, experience, and personality; and 500 points are on the basis of examinations. The examinations are divided into "general" and "special" examinations. The "general" examination, given to all teachers and designed to measure the qualifications common to all members of the teaching profession, includes (1) general education and culture; (2) general professional information; and (3) academic aptitude. The "special" examination consists of a major and at least one minor in teaching fields selected by the candidate. The scores of all examinations are translated into percentile ratings and added to provide a total rating. When the final group ratings and examination rating have been obtained, they are combined; and candidates are selected in the order of their combined rating within the subject classification.

Regardless of the various systems used in rating and weighting the written examinations in the different cities, those responsible for teacher selection are endeavoring (1) to secure anonymity, (2) to secure a score (or grade or rating) that is as objective as they deem it possible to secure under the local conditions, (3) to make possible a graded eligible list of successful candidates, (4) to eliminate undesirable and inefficient teachers, (5) to secure a score (or grade or rating) which attempts to evaluate the abilities and training of the individual candidate in terms of similar abilities and training of other candidates, and (6) to make possible the appointment and assignment of teachers upon the basis of merit ascertained as far as their procedures make it practicable. Since it is held that the written examination as a procedure in teacher selection is very limited and need not be a necessary requirement, it is not the purpose of this study to make any recommendations as to the method of rating or weighting such examination.

CHAPTER VII

ESTABLISHING MINIMUM QUALIFICATIONS FOR TEACHING

IN ORDER to be eligible to receive assignment or appointment to teaching positions, to take teachers' examinations, or to obtain certificates to teach, candidates must fulfill certain minimum requirements. For the most part these requirements include such factors as training, both educational and professional, age, and experience.

MINIMUM TRAINING REQUIREMENTS

It is becoming increasingly necessary to establish minimum training requirements or educational qualifications for all teachers. Teaching service demands a trained, competent teaching personnel, and the state or local community has the right to prescribe the desirable minimum standards.[1] Moreover, the growing complexity of American life, the demands of specialization, the advancement in the various fields of knowledge, and the development of the science of education have compelled the establishment of minimum training requirements or general and professional educational qualifications.[2] All of the cities included in this study have set up minimum requirements for the different educational levels, but they vary considerably. Graduation from an approved four-year high school course, or its equivalent, and the graduation from an approved normal or professional school for teachers whose course of study shall be not less than two years, has been set as the minimum requirement for elementary teaching positions in twenty-four of the thirty-seven cities. Seven cities require three years of training beyond high school graduation, and six systems require four years of post-high school education.

Where there are junior high schools or intermediate schools, the minimum requirement of an approved four-year college course prevails. However, there are four cities which have established three years of college or university work as the minimum. In the high

[1] Buckingham, B. R., *Supply and Demand in Teacher Training*, p. 156. 1926.
[2] Criterion XIV, p. 21.

school and senior high school fields, thirty-one of the cities require four full years of training above the high school in a standard college or university. One city has set three years of college or university training as the minimum; and five cities have made five years beyond high school graduation the training requirement.

In view of the fact that graduation from a standard college or university does not of itself always indicate that the applicant has had adequate specific academic preparation, an attempt has been made in some of the systems to establish certain academic requirements for junior and senior high school positions in terms of semester hours in "major" and "minor" specialization fields. Two cities have established a minimum requirement of at least twelve semester hours in the major subject; eleven cities, eighteen semester hours; three cities, twenty-four semester hours; and two cities, thirty semester hours. Likewise, five cities have established a minimum requirement of at least ten semester hours in the minor subject; four cities, twelve semester hours; and two cities, eighteen semester hours.

With respect to professional preparation or courses in education, the normal school or teacher-training programs include courses to meet the minimum requirements for elementary grade positions. In the junior and senior high school fields, however, some of the systems have found it necessary to require that a definite number of semester hours in education be included as part of the educational training of the candidate. Three cities have established a minimum of twelve semester hours in education; eight cities, fifteen semester hours; five cities, from seventeen to nineteen semester hours; twelve cities, eighteen semester hours; one city, twenty semester hours; and two cities, twenty-four semester hours. It is interesting to note that many of the school systems have definitely listed the names or types of professional courses or courses in education which will be accepted or which must be offered as part of the minimum training requirements. Table IX gives the professional courses which are found most frequently mentioned.

"EQUIVALENT" REQUIREMENTS

These minimum educational requirements do not always apply, however, in some of the largest cities where the candidates are seek-

TABLE IX

PROFESSIONAL COURSES REQUIRED AS PART OF MINIMUM
TRAINING QUALIFICATIONS

Name of Course Required	Number of Cities Requiring
Psychology: General, Educational.	25
Observation and Practice Teaching.	22
Methods of Teaching: General, Special.	19
Principles of Teaching.	10
Principles of Secondary Education.	8
History of Education.	7
Principles and Techniques of High School Teaching.	6
Administration, Organization, or Management of the Secondary School	6

ing positions as special subject teachers. In view of local conditions, it has been the practice often to permit such candidates to furnish evidence of scholarship, in whole or in part, equivalent to that of a graduate of a normal school or a college; and in addition show proficiency in the special department or subject for which the application is made. Equivalents in terms of approved, practical, or trade experience and of approved special courses are accepted in lieu of the standard number of years of preparation beyond high school graduation. The "equivalents" have been deemed necessary because the various teacher-training institutions have not, until recently, been so organized that they could prepare their students adequately for such special teaching positions. However, as these institutions are gradually offering students definite curricula for special teachers and are broadening the opportunities for extension work in these fields, the qualifications for all teachers will approach uniformity in the respective fields and the necessity to include "equivalents" will gradually disappear. A few examples of equivalent qualifications for special teachers are submitted:

Applicants for positions as teachers in special departments, such as vocal music, freehand drawing, mechanical drawing, manual training, home economics, and physical training, will be required to furnish evidence of scholarship equivalent to that of a graduate of a normal school, and in addition, must show proficiency in the special department for which application is made. (Birmingham)

In the case of teachers of art, music, commerce, physical education, library practice, and industrial arts, certificates issued by approved institutions and covering four years of study equivalent in grade and in amount to a four-year college course may be accepted as the equivalent of a college degree; provided, further, that in the cases of the subjects enumerated, two years of approved post-high school education and four years of approved experience in the respective fields may be accepted in lieu of the college work or its equivalent; and provided, further, that in the case of teachers of industrial arts, eight years of approved training or experience, including at least two years of practical experience, may be accepted in lieu of the college degree or its equivalent. (Philadelphia)

Candidates for positions as teachers of special subjects must present credentials showing special preparation and experience; in addition, they must pass an examination in the subjects they are to teach, and in Pedagogy, including Methods and Principles of Teaching, English Language and Literature, and United States History. (Kansas City)

In the case of subjects other than academic, equivalents in terms of approved, practical, or "trade" experience, may be accepted in the ratio of two years of such experience to one year of education; provided, however, that under no schedule shall the maximum of such "equivalents" exceed one year less than the number of years beyond high school required as standard by the position in question. (Cleveland)

One year or more of approved practical trade experience may be accepted in lieu of one year of technical training, so that one year of professional training above the high school and one year of approved practical experience may be considered the equivalent of the minimum professional training required. (Denver)

Teachers of commercial or industrial subjects may secure their advanced standing in an academic, commercial, or technical school of recognized standing; or they may offer a limited amount of trade experience in lieu of advanced educational training. It shall require two years of trade experience to count as one year of academic training; and not more than one-half of the advanced training requirements may be gained in a trade. (Minneapolis)

The minimum qualifications for teachers of shopwork and mechanical drawing are as follows:

1. Graduation from an approved trade school, secondary technical school or engineering school of college grade and completed apprenticeship experience, and 240 hours of teacher training work, or
2. Elementary school education of eight grades and at least two years' journey-man experience beyond apprenticeship in the trade which he is to teach, and 240 hours of teacher-training work. (Baltimore)

Requirements for Teachers of High School Industrial Arts Subjects:

1. Graduation from a high school, or an equivalent academic education, the completion of a two-year day industrial teacher-training course and three years of teaching experience, or

2. Graduation from a high school or an equivalent academic education and five years' journey-man experience in the subject in which the applicant seeks a license, together with (*a*) 480 hours of approved industrial teacher-training work or (*b*) completion of an approved one-year day industrial teacher-training course; or

3. Graduation from an approved four-year college course in engineering or architecture together with 480 hours of approved industrial teacher-training work, which may have been concurrent with the college course; or

4. The completion of two years of approved work in a college of engineering or architecture, two years of practical experience in the subject in which the applicant seeks a license, and 480 hours of approved industrial teacher-training work. (New York)

These "equivalents" for minimum educational qualifications include (1) experience in the trade or vocation, either as master mechanic or craftsman, journeyman, or apprentice; (2) certification of approved special courses; (3) a specified number of semester hours of teacher-training work; (4) satisfactory evidence of proficiency in the special department or subject; (5) teaching experience; or (6) a combination of several types of "equivalents."

Summary and Conclusions

In order that any school system may secure adequately prepared teachers, it is mandatory that those responsible for teacher selection formulate definite minimum training qualifications which must be met by the candidates.[3] These qualifications should be of such standard that it would be impossible for those to be considered for teaching positions who do not, by their training and professional preparation, give evidence of being well qualified. Considering the practices in these thirty-seven cities and the weight of educational authorities, those responsible for the establishment of minimum training qualifications should base their program on the following recommendations:

[3] Criterion XIV, p. 21.

1. Definite requirements as to academic and professional training should be set up for every position for which teachers are employed.

2. These requirements should include general academic training, specific training in the special field of work for which the candidate has applied, and professional training.

3. There is no evidence to justify a recommendation that elementary teachers should have less professional training or less pre-service preparation than secondary school teachers. In fact, "Teachers in kindergarten and elementary schools should be as well prepared (in point of time required for pre-service preparation) as teachers in secondary schools. This recommendation implies that standards for kindergarten and elementary teachers should be increased and not that secondary standards should be lowered." [4]

4. At least a minimum of four years of professional preparation beyond high school should be established as a requirement for all teachers.[5] Superintendents throughout the country have recommended that "every state should set the goal of four or more years above high school at some date in the near future." [6]

5. Where local conditions make it necessary to require higher training qualifications for secondary school teachers, a minimum of five years of pre-service preparation should be required for secondary school teachers. This recommendation is in line with the growing belief that such teachers should be upgraded to a minimum of one year of graduate work.[7] Certainly for this longer period of preparation there is precedent in the thoroughgoing preparation of secondary school teachers in Germany, France, England, and in a few cities of the United States.[8]

6. The importance of well-qualified teachers in our program of public education makes it desirable that the best teacher preparation

[4] National Survey of the Education of Teachers, Vol. II: *Teacher Personnel in the United States,* p. 104.

[5] National Education Association, Department of Superintendence, *Official Report,* "Report of the Committee on Resolutions," p. 302. 1936.

[6] *Teacher Personnel in the United States,* p. 104.

[7] National Education Association, Department of Superintendence, *Official Report, op. cit.,* p. 302. 1936.

[8] National Survey of the Education of Teachers, Vol. III: *Teacher Education Curricula,* p. 313.

be the minimum requirement. Many educators are of the opinion that a four-year period of college preparation with high standards of proficiency should be established as a prerequisite to professional preparation. Even though the National Survey of the Education of Teachers recommends a minimum of four years of college preparation for elementary teachers and five years for secondary teachers, this period of training seems all too short to train teachers in the three important phases of teacher preparation—general cultural education, specialized material to be taught, and the distinctly professional elements concerned with the teaching procedures in curricular and extracurricular activities. A more reasonable organization of this period of preparation would be four years of general collegiate study to provide a broad type of cultural liberal background upon which to build a two or three years' strictly professional preparation at the graduate level.

AGE REQUIREMENTS

Boards of education and teacher-selecting agencies have realized the necessity for some age limitations with reference to applicants for teaching positions. No one desires to assign or appoint a teacher who is not fully matured or who is incapable of commanding respect because of lack of maturity. On the other hand, no system, as a general policy, cares to employ teachers who have reached an age which bars them from further growth and development in the profession and which may make them a poor investment in terms of years of future service. This latter consideration is held even more important in those systems which operate under tenure and retirement laws, and some types of salary schedules.

A few of the systems represented in this study have established both lower and upper age limits for applicants. For example, one city (Buffalo) rules that no person shall be eligible to teach who is under eighteen years and no candidate can be considered who is over forty years of age. Another city (New Orleans) follows the policy of appointing no applicant not already in the service of the board of education to any principalship or teaching position who is under eighteen years or over fifty years of age. Two eastern cities (Jersey City and Newark) have the same age limits, eighteen years and forty-five years; while several others (such as Los Angeles, Kansas City, and Birmingham) have established nineteen years as the lower limit. The general requirements for applicants in another city (New York) read that no person, unless in his case the board of education suspends the by-laws regarding the age limits, is eligible to enter an examination for license as a teacher in high school who is not over twenty-one and less than forty-one years of age, on the last date set for the receipt of applications.

While in most of the cities the age of the teaching group is controlled at the lowest level by a limitation of eighteen years, the basic eligibility requirements covering academic and professional training are tending more or less to set a lower age limit somewhat above the general practice. For example, where a city (Washington) requires a bachelor's degree from an accredited teachers college following a four-year professional course; or where a master's degree is required for a high school teaching position (as in Boston), the lower age limit is certainly extended or automatically raised. The same situation arises where a three-year normal course is required; or where systems have fixed the lower age limit for entrance to their normal schools or teacher-training institutions and require the satisfactory completion of a three- or four-year course of study.

Practically all the cities have established an upper age limit which varies from thirty-five to fifty years of age. The following illustrate the various types of regulations fixing such limits:

Only in exceptional cases will a teacher whose age is more than thirty-five be appointed. (Denver)

Applicants must not have passed the fortieth birthday on the last day before filing application. (San Francisco)

No one over forty-nine years of age may be certificated. (Chicago)

At the time of appointment the candidate will not be over the age limit prescribed for teacherships as follows: All senior and junior high school teacherships, forty-five years; all other teacherships, forty years. (Washington)

No certificate qualifying the permanent appointment as a member of the supervisory staff or as a teacher in the public schools shall remain valid after the thirty-first day of December next following the fortieth birthday of the holder thereof, provided, that this age limitation shall not apply to teachers or members of the supervisory staff who are already in the permanent school service. (Boston)

No person who has reached the age of fifty years shall receive initial appointment in the Department of Instruction, and no person shall be restored to service in that department who has reached the age of fifty-five years. (Philadelphia)

A candidate must be under forty-five years of age. (Kansas City)

It shall be the general policy of the Board of Education to elect young teachers. (Atlanta)

It is quite evident that school systems have attempted by setting up age qualifications to protect their schools against immaturity on the part of teachers. At the same time they have also endeavored to keep out of their schools those applicants who have reached an age which may render them undesirable risks as initial appointments or which offers little or no hope for further professional growth. These limits are expressions of administrative policies and reflect not only practice elsewhere and experience, but also local conditions, tenure, and salary schedules.

The establishment of minimum educational qualifications will undoubtedly set the lower age limits for entering teachers. Naturally, any tendency to raise those qualifications by increasing the length of the pre-service preparation will automatically raise the age limit. If a minimum of four years of professional training be set up for all teachers, the minimum age limit will become twenty or twenty-one years. The other end of the picture presents a different story. How old can an applicant be before he is refused initial appointment in a school system? Practice differs, although forty to forty-five years seems to be the upper limit set by most of the largest cities. In view of the operation of tenure laws and salary schedules which tend to discourage the appointment of teachers beyond the age of forty, and considering the desirability of having a staff of teachers representing an advantageous spread in terms of age, as well as in years of experience, it is good administration to avoid those limitations that will prohibit the initial appointment of relatively young teachers or encourage the applications of those who at best have only a comparatively few years of excellent service and professional growth to offer.

Previous teaching experience as a necessary qualification for appointment or assignment is not a uniform requirement in our large city systems, although such requirement is more common with respect to high school positions than in the case of elementary or grade school positions. In those systems which have their own municipally controlled normal schools or teacher-training institutions, or which are closely allied with similar state institutions, previous teaching experience is not a requisite for assignment to elementary school positions. In such institutions the candidates have received a type of training which includes adequate courses in observation and practice teaching under very careful guidance and supervision. Often, this guidance and supervision is either under the direction of the city school administration or subject to its inspection and approval. However, six of the cities in this study do require previous experience for elementary positions. Two of these require at least one year of "successful teaching experience" and four have established two years of teaching experience as a minimum requirement.

For positions in both the junior and the senior high school grades more than half of the cities definitely require previous training experience. Four of them require one year of teaching experience, thirteen require two years, and three require three years as a minimum qualification. For example, one city (Detroit) notifies its applicants that no person may receive a contract to teach any academic subject in the high schools who has not had at least one year of teaching experience in a town or city school system. Another city (Seattle) requires for both junior and senior high school positions at least one year's successful teaching experience in a high or junior high school, and adds a further condition that teachers elected with but one year's experience begin at one step below the regular minimum salary. The board of education in another city (Atlanta) has ruled that no person shall be employed as a teacher in the junior and senior high schools who does not hold a baccalaureate degree from a standard college and who has not had in addition at least two years of successful experience in junior or senior high school work. A similar requirement in another system (Minneapolis) reads as follows:

For appointment, a teacher must have had two years of experience as a teacher, under competent supervision in schools recognized by the state as accredited schools or schools of equal standing in other states. Experience should have been terminated not more than three years before the date upon which the contract is issued.

Another example is to be found in an eastern city (Jersey City) where the requirements for the certificate to teach in the high schools include "at least three years' experience in teaching or supervision."

Even where the boards of education have definitely established minimum requirements in terms of previous teaching experience, applicants are generally notified that preference will be given those possessing qualifications beyond such minimum requirements. This is especially true in the case of applicants for high school positions; and as a result, applicants with more than the one, two, or three years of previous teaching experience are selected.

In those systems where previous teaching experience is not required, the boards of education have established alternative qualifications which permit years of teaching experience to be substituted for deficiencies in the professional training of the candidate. Two examples are sufficient to illustrate this practice. In one system (Buffalo) candidates must present evidence of the successful completion of eighteen semester hours in courses of education approved by the board of examiners as pedagogical in character or evidence of two years of successful teaching experience. In another system (Milwaukee) three years of preparation beyond high school graduation are required of all candidates for positions as teacher in the elementary school. However, a year of successful experience may be substituted for the third year of preparation.

Likewise, provisions are made in some systems to substitute additional educational and professional training for a portion of the required teaching experience. For example, one city (Boston) has provided that a degree from the Teachers College of the City of Boston, the Master's Degree in Education earned prior to September 1, 1928, under the plan approved by the Board of Superintendents, or the Master's Degree in Education from a college or university approved by the Board of Superintendents with educational courses approved by the Board, may be accepted as equivalent to one of the three years required in teaching and governing regular graded day schools. On the other hand, one city has definitely ruled against any substitution of teaching experience for other requirements.

> However, no amount of experience can be substituted for the required academic and professional training, nor for the required examination. (Baltimore)

Arguments For and Against Experience Requirements

In the elementary field the question of "required experience" is not a serious one since it affects so few of the cities. In the secondary field, however, the problem becomes more acute. Whether the practice is justified or not depends largely upon the point of view. The significant arguments in favor of requiring teaching experience are as follows:

1. School systems which can afford to pay higher salaries are entitled to superior teaching service which might be expected from experienced teachers.

2. The requirement will automatically check the hundreds of yearly applications of those just graduating from the teacher-training institutions without any experience.

3. The employment of experienced teachers simplifies the supervisory and in-service training of teachers.

4. The requirement eliminates those applicants who have not been successful in their teaching experience elsewhere and who cannot secure satisfactory recommendations concerning such experience.

To offset these favorable statements, there are several important reactions against the practice of requiring experience for initial employment. These are:

1. The practice of demanding teaching experience gained at the expense of less favored communities is certainly at odds with the fundamental theory that education is a function of the state and conducted for the greatest good of all the people.

2. From the standpoint of sound state administration, smaller and less wealthy communities should not be robbed of their best teachers because of higher salaries available in larger and wealthier communities.

3. The experience requirement leads to a practice which is harmful to the teaching profession—"promotion by moving." "The fact that so many of our public school teachers expect to obtain their 'promotion'

by moving instead of by unusually meritorious work in a permanent position is one of the greatest obstacles in the recognition of teaching as a profession." [9]

4. The experience requirement handicaps the work of the teacher-training institutions which cannot devote time necessary to the complete preparation of prospective teachers for the work they will eventually follow. These institutions too often must think in terms of a shorter preparation period in order to have their students ready to teach in the smaller and less favored communities so that they can get their one, two, or three years of experience.

5. Another objection to the experience requirement is that the experience thus gained is not necessarily the most desirable or of real benefit to the school system which employs on that basis. At best, the benefit is often very small. It is quite likely that these early, most important, habit-forming classroom experiences are secured in school situations which are in no way comparable with what the teacher will meet in the new position. As has been often said, "Practice does not make perfect unless it is the right kind of practice." It stands to reason that experience gained in poorly supervised and unprofessionally administered schools does not guarantee superior teaching ability.

"Rather than select a teacher whose previous experience has been outside the scope of his prospective position, the school authorities might better appoint an inexperienced recruit with excellent training, and let him obtain his first experience under competent supervision in the field he is expected to teach." [10]

Summary and Conclusions

The solution to this problem is again to be found in the professional cooperation of school authorities and educational leaders in our cities and the teacher-training institutions. School systems can and should demand and secure adequate initial preparation of all new teachers. Standards covering selection of recruits for training, academic and professional training, observation and practice teaching can be and should be uniformly established, rigidly enforced, and professionally up-graded; but previous teaching experience as a

[9] Evenden, E. S., "The Superintendent of Schools and the Education of Teachers," p. 207. *Official Report of the Department of Superintendence,* National Education Association, Atlantic City, February 23–28, 1935.

[10] National Education Association, "Administrative Practices Affecting Classroom Teachers," Part I: The Selection and Appointment of Teachers. *Research Bulletin,* Vol. X, No. 1, p. 26.

necessary qualification need not be and cannot be required in every program of teacher selection.[11]

ELIGIBILITY OF MARRIED WOMEN

The eligibility of married women for assignment or appointment as regular teachers is recognized and accepted in twenty-nine of the thirty-seven cities studied. They can be employed as teachers on precisely the same basis as single women as to appointment, salaries, and promotion. Of the eight cities barring married women, several have made exceptions for a few special cases. For example, in one city (San Francisco) married women are not eligible for the competitive examinations unless their husbands are totally incapacitated through disease or infirmity, such incapacity to be certified by the board of health. Another exception is noted (Buffalo) where no married woman shall be permitted to take the examinations unless evidence of legal separation is furnished. In a third city (Jersey City) any married woman who proves to the satisfaction of the board of education that, because of her husband's mental or physical illness, she is entirely dependent upon her own labor for her support, and who complies with the requirements of rules governing the issuance of certificates, may be appointed assistant teacher.

Most of the cities which do not appoint married women to regular positions further rule that the marriage of a woman employed in a teaching position shall constitute a resignation or automatically terminate the contract of such teacher without further notice. One city (Jersey City) has this restriction apply only during the probationary period. Should a woman teacher marry during the three years of her probation service as a teacher, the position shall thereupon become vacant. Another city (Atlanta), which declares married teachers eligible for appointment, notifies its teachers approaching maternity to resign. A similar ruling is in force in Indianapolis where the teaching contract of a teacher who during the term of the contract is or becomes an expectant mother shall automatically terminate not later than four months prior to her confinement. The board of education in one of the largest cities (Cleveland) explains its policy as follows:

[11] Criterion XV, p. 22.

In itself the marital relations of a teacher of either sex shall not be treated as a bar to regular appointment, but the continuance in service for the remainder of the school year for which she is appointed of a woman teacher who marries after receiving a regular appointment shall be subject to the recommendation of the Superintendent of Schools and the approval of the Board of Education.

Where the eligibility of married women is recognized and accepted, it is required by the educational authorities that women teachers who marry send immediate information to the superintendent's office, giving the date of marriage and the change of name.

Summary and Conclusions

In some states court decisions as well as rulings by state boards of education have clearly stated that marriage in itself does not constitute any reasonable bar against teaching and should in no way affect the status of the teacher in the school. Certainly if teachers are to be selected on the basis of merit and efficient preparation, and since research has not disclosed any sound reason to support a definite discrimination against married teachers, then the question of the marital status of the applicant should not be a factor in teacher selection.[12] In the few cases where court decisions have been made, only two issues have been settled:

Marriage in itself is not a valid cause for the removal of a teacher who is under contract.

Where a teacher is under "tenure," which very definitely enumerates specific causes or charges for the removal of a teacher, marriage in itself does not constitute one of those specific causes for removal.

These two issues do not restrict the right of any board of education to refuse employment to a married woman. Local conditions will affect administrative policies, but professional policies dealing with the selection of teachers will aim to secure and retain efficient, well-qualified teachers and to eliminate those who are inefficient; and superintendents and their agencies will administer those policies on a merit basis, and with impartiality to all applicants without regard to the marital status.

[12] Criterion XV, p. 22.

CHAPTER VIII

VERIFYING AND EVALUATING THE CANDIDATE'S CREDENTIALS

AFTER the candidate has submitted or indicated sufficient and satisfactory evidence of meeting the minimum qualifications for the position for which he has applied, the selecting agency must properly evaluate the relative merit of such fitness. Careful examination and verification of all credentials and other records are first necessary; then a uniform rating must follow.[1] The procedure may vary according to local conditions and types of organization; yet in order to conform with the principle that selection be made on a merit basis,[2] the selecting agency is required to set up an acceptable uniform method for evaluating and rating the qualifications of each candidate.

VERIFICATION OF CREDENTIALS

Every city represented in this study has set up definite educational qualifications which establish a required minimum of both general and professional education which candidates must satisfy before they can be considered qualified, ready for a personal interview, or eligible for any competitive examination. Certified evidence of such training and preparation is necessary or must be made available. In a majority of the cities the candidate is required only to list his general education and professional training, giving names of institutions and dates attended; courses and specialized fields; degrees, diplomas, and credits earned; and date of graduation. The agency in charge of teacher selection has the responsibility of sending to the respective institutions for certified records. One city (New York) compels the candidate to fill out and swear to an affidavit that all statements in his application, to the best of his knowledge and belief, are complete and accurate. Other cities, however, include on their

[1] Criterion VII, p. 16.
[2] Criterion II, p. 13.

128

application blanks or circulars of information a statement to the effect that false statements on the part of any candidate will forfeit all rights and privileges otherwise due the candidate.

Nine of the cities demand that certified transcripts of high school and normal school, college, or university records accompany the application. These certified statements must show the courses taken, credits received, and marks or grades given. Two cities ask the candidate to have the college or university submit to the board of examiners or the superintendent the certified statements of the candidate's credits. In those cities where state certificates are required, either the state certificate or a statement of credit evaluation from the state department of education must be submitted.

EVALUATION OF CREDENTIALS

In keeping with the principle of merit, there remains the important problem of evaluating the relative merits of the credentials after they have been verified. Some cities establish a minimum eligibility requirement or accept a state certificate and use it as the only factor in rating the training and preparation of the candidate. These minimum requirements are stated with all possible clearness and must be met. Substitution of apparently equivalent qualifications cannot be permitted. This practice is found in some of the cities where competitive examinations are held. Other cities, however, have found it desirable to provide means of rating the qualifications so that academic and professional training beyond the minimum requirements can be evaluated and those candidates with higher or distinctly superior type of training can be so rated.

Practices in the Larger Cities

In a few cities a careful inspection of credentials and certified transcripts of educational and professional training separates the candidates into two groups, (1) those who merely qualify, and (2) those who have superior qualifications. The latter are given a preferred listing. One city (Cincinnati) goes a step further and requires that candidates who are given a preferred listing must have a scholarship record indicating at least a "B" average in educational training and in the teaching field, and a "C" average in general academic work. Cleveland notifies candidates that a strong preference will be given those having educational qualifications beyond standard requirements. In Seattle the credentials of the applicants are arranged according to the preference of grade or subject listed, and rated separately by at least three examiners. The ratings of the individual examiners are not known until all have been submitted and an average of the ratings has been made by the superintendent's office. The credentials of each applicant are rated according to the following system: the highest rank is 1, the next lower 1—; then 2+, 2, 2—; 3+, 3, 3—, etc. These ratings, however, evaluate not only the educational and professional training, but also the experience and confidential reports concerning personality, ability, and success of the applicant as a teacher.

In several cities, where all competitive examinations are evaluated on a basis of a total number of points, the complete examination is divided into several divisions or parts and each division or part is given credit for so many points. This procedure gives opportunity for evaluating and rating all factors considered, including educational and professional training as well as experience. In one of these cities (San Francisco) the complete examination consists of four sections, with a total evaluation of 1000 points. Under one section the candidate is rated on the "amount of college or university training," with a possible score of 130 points. Under another section he is rated on the "quality of training (college rating)," with a possible score of 300 points. A prescribed number of points is granted for the minimum requirements and additional points are given for advanced work or extra courses. This rating is done by members of the department of personnel. In rating the "quality of training," the department asks the institutions in which the applicants have been trained to rate them on a five-point scale. A specified number of points is assigned to each step on this scale.

In another city (Boston), where the complete examination records are evaluated on the basis of 1000 points, applicants who submit evidence of only the required amount of education and experience and who submit satisfactory credentials in regard to their teaching experience, are given the credit of 70 points for what is termed a "satisfactory minimum." A further credit is allowed, up to ten points, for education in excess of the minimum requirements. An additional credit of ten points is allowed for extra experience, and another credit of ten points for what may be called "superior evidence of teaching ability." The additional credit for experience is measured by allowing two points per year up to and including five years beyond the standard requirement of two years.

A third city in this group (Pittsburgh) evaluates the examination records on the basis of 100 points. The board of examiners gives a possible total of 60 points to the evaluation of official transcripts of academic and professional records, teaching experience, and observed teaching. A similar practice is followed in a fourth city (Providence), where the rating of a candidate is based on a thousand points. Of the 1000 possible points which a candidate may earn to determine his final rating, 200 points are given to the rating of training and experience. These include such elements as (1) education and practice teaching, (2) actual teaching experience, and (3) any other experiences that should be valuable as a foundation for successful teaching.

A somewhat different method of evaluating credentials is being followed in one of our largest systems (Washington). In the first place, only those courses or degrees receive extra credit which are in excess of the eligibility requirements to take the competitive examinations. Claim sheets are filled out by the candidates and filed with the board of examiners together with the supporting specified evidence. The number of credits used as the basis of evaluating every item on the claim sheets is the maximum number obtainable. Courses in education and courses in subject matter, over and above eligibility, taken within the past fifteen years, are given extra credits. For example, on one claim sheet five credits were allowable on each subject matter or content course, with a possible maximum of 80 credits for all subject matter courses. On the same claim sheet a total of 140 credits were assigned to courses in education. Graduate courses were allowed a maximum of ten credits each and undergraduate courses, a maximum of seven credits each. Such courses in education were classified into four groups and a maximum number of courses allowed in each group. Recorded success in teaching is likewise evaluated in terms of credits. The rating is determined by five official discriminating scores, with consideration given only to the marks "ES" exceptionally superior (valued at 50 credits); "E" excellent (valued at 40 credits); and "VG" very good (valued at 30 credits).

Another of our largest cities (Chicago) uses a 100-point scale which provides for the evaluation of the minimum as well as the maximum training and experience. The minimum qualifications are given a value of 40 points. Extra points are given for additional training with a maximum value of 25 points, distributed as follows:

> For study courses in addition to a bachelor's degree, 1 point for each major of three semester hours, graduate or undergraduate work, up to 10 points.
>
> For advanced work in the candidate's special subject or major up to 10 points. (This work must be beyond the minimum of five college majors.)
>
> For courses in Education, 1 point for each major, graduate or undergraduate work, up to 5 points.

In addition the quality of the education training is evaluated and a maximum of 10 points given. This evaluation is based on the general scholastic average made by the candidate and the points allotted are as follows:

> C average equals two points
> C+ or B— average equals four points
> B average equals six points
> B+ or A— average equals eight points
> A average equals ten points

Experience is also evaluated, two points being given for each year of experience with the total maximum points limited to twenty, and an extra five points allowed for outstanding success in teaching. An "age penalty" is included in this scale whereby a deduction of one point is made for each year over forty years, with a limit of ten points.

Another method for evaluating credentials, involving the use of a series of scales of points, has been followed in St. Louis. The rating of the applicant is based on the total scores or points made on five separate items:

> 1. Specific training represented by the number of college credits in the special field of study for which the applicant applied.

2. Professional training represented by the number of credits in the field of Education.

3. General training represented by the sum of all other college and university credits.

4. Experience in teaching.

5. Age (at last birthday).

These five items are selected for two reasons. In the first place, they are purely objective, and the first three are very readily determined by certified transcripts from the colleges and universities. In the second place, they are basic items generally considered in the selection of teachers. In determining the exact scale of values for credits in the first four items listed, the board of education has considered the principle of diminishing returns. The scale of points awarded to semester hours in both "specific training in special subject" and "professional training" establishes 100 points as the maximum, with the number of points diminishing after the first thirty hours. For example, thirty hours will rate 30 points on the scale; sixty hours, 45 points; ninety hours, 52½ points. The scale of points for "general study" also gives 100 points as the maximum, but with points diminishing after the first sixty hours. For example, sixty hours will rate 60 points; ninety hours, 75 points; one hundred and twenty hours, 82½ points; one hundred and fifty hours, 86¼ points. The scale of points for "experience" is based on 24 points, diminishing somewhat after the third year of experience and very rapidly after the ninth year. For example, 12 points are given for three years of experience; 18 points for six years; 21 points for nine years; and approximately 22 points for twenty years. The scale for the fifth item, "age," is purely an indication of the administrative policy of the school system. It awards the maximum of ten points to applicants between the ages of thirty and forty years, but gives a zero rating for those twenty-five years of age or younger as well as for those forty-five or older.

It is to be noted that these various scales do not take into consideration the scholastic standing or the qualitative difference in college credits as shown by the applicant's marks or grades. Such qualitative differences are recognized, however, and indirectly evaluated by the oral examining committee. A committee of examiners is appointed to meet each applicant, and each examiner makes an individual report upon the general fitness of the applicant for the position. Consideration is given to both the examiners' reports and the total point rating in determining the final standing of the applicant for appointment or assignment.

Purpose of the Evaluation

From the analysis of the practices in the various cities, credentials are evaluated for four purposes:

1. To satisfy the minimum or desirable qualifications.
2. To rate the applicant's preparation and other qualifications on a percentage or credit value basis, to be used in listing the applicant as a "preferred" candidate.
3. To rate the applicant's preparation and other qualification on a percentage or credit value basis, such rating to be combined with ratings on other procedures (personal interview, teaching test, written examination) in order to obtain a final or general rating of the applicant.
4. To accomplish (1) and either (2) or (3).

Methods of Evaluation

Moreover, practice clearly indicates that these credentials are evaluated in any of the following ways:

1. By mere personal judgment of one examiner.
2. By separate personal judgments of two or more examiners, and the several ratings averaged.
3. On the basis of number of semester hours or courses or degrees or years of study beyond the minimum or desirable requirements.
4. By giving extra value or credits or points to high scholastic attainments represented by certain designated college marks or grades or ratings.
5. By giving a number of points or credits for a satisfactory minimum and allowing extra points or credits for advanced preparation, training, experience, etc. (A maximum allowance is usually set for these extra points or credits.)

As for the types of credentials evaluated, the various practices list the following which can be supported by documentary evidence:

1. Specific training in the special field of study.
2. Professional training in the field of education.
3. General training.
4. General academic studies.
5. Scholarship record or averages.
6. College rating (general).
7. Confidential reports concerning personality, ability, training, and success as a teacher.
8. Observed teaching, where supervisory reports are available.
9. Experience.
10. Superior evidence of teaching experience.
11. Age.

It is recognized among school authorities that the amount and character of academic and professional training is a good measure of the applicant's preparation.[3] However, the individual who evaluates such credentials will consider (a) the nature and value of the courses which are offered as preparation for the particular position for which the applicant has applied; (b) the general scholastic ranking throughout the period of preparation; (c) the professional standing of the institutions in which the training was acquired; and (d) the professional attitude developed by the applicant as far as the continuity of the training program and the extent of specialization can indicate it.

Summary and Conclusions

Since other reliable measures have not been devised, the quality and quantity of training can be advantageously used as one index of the applicant's preparation and fitness for the particular teaching position. The certification by accredited teacher-training institutions may profitably be accepted and used in the program of teacher selection. Accordingly, the following recommendations concerning credentials and their evaluation are suggested as part of any well-planned program of teacher selection:

[3] *Official Report of the Educational Survey Commission, State of Florida*, p. 182.

1. Credentials should be full, complete documentary evidence covering those general items for which the local board of education has established minimum or desirable requirements.

2. Such credentials should be from accredited, approved, accepted, or responsible sources.

3. All credentials should be first evaluated or checked in order to ascertain whether the applicant has satisfied the minimum or reasonable requirements established by the local board of education for the particular position for which the application has been made.

4. The credentials of those applicants who have met the minimum or desirable requirements should then be studied and evaluated in order to determine the superior qualifications of any one applicant as compared with the qualifications of all the other applicants for the same position.

5. A type of grading system should be used whereby training and preparation beyond the minimum or desirable requirements in (*a*) general academic training, (*b*) specific training in the special field of training, and (*c*) professional training, can be credited. Certain maximum limits should be a part of the grading system based on a study of the teaching personnel in the system, the principle of diminishing returns, and any local situations which might condition it.

6. The type of grading system should be so devised that it will give a decided recognition to the qualitative differences in the training of applicants as shown by their general scholastic average in each of (*a*), (*b*), and (*c*) in (5) above.

7. If "age" limitations are definitely established as a requirement, and no one is to be employed who is under or over the age limits, there appears no just reason to include the item "age" for evaluation. Ordinarily the specifications and desirable qualifications for any particular position can very well stipulate a lower age range or an upper age range. Moreover, the rating as the result of a personal interview or the teaching test can consider the element of "age" as it affects the applicant's fitness for the specific position. The same consideration can be given to the item "experience." The confidential reports, which are in a sense documentary, are difficult to evaluate and grade. They should be carefully examined and accepted as "satisfactory," "doubtful," or "unsatisfactory"; but they do not

seem to be part of the training credentials. Moreover, the personal interview and the teaching test will in all probability consider the elements found in the "satisfactory" testimonials. The "doubtful" and the "unsatisfactory" testimonials would bar the applicant until all doubt and unsatisfactory qualifications have been removed.

8. The rating of the applicant resulting from a carefully planned evaluation of credentials should play an important part in the final or general rating.

CHAPTER IX

ASSIGNING OR APPOINTING THE CANDIDATE, ELIGIBLE LISTS, AND PROBATIONARY SERVICE

IF THE program of teacher selection provides means of carefully investigating and uniformly evaluating the qualifications of acceptable candidates; and if all assignments and appointments are to be made on the basis of merit thus ascertained,[1] it follows that the names of those candidates who meet all requirements should be listed under proper classifications and in order of rank or standing.[2] Such lists of eligibles serve to protect the selecting agency against charges of non-educational influences or personal favoritism and to guarantee the school system, within the limitations of its program of selection, an available supply of properly qualified eligibles. At the same time such lists tend to demand the continuous exercise of professional procedures in eliminating the undesirable candidates and in segregating those whose complete qualifications rank them at the top. But being placed on an eligible list should not mean a guarantee of assignment or appointment. Such placement notifies the successful applicant that he is eligible to consideration for assignment in comparison to all others on the list. Often the successful candidate feels that because his name is on the eligible list, he has established priority rights, regardless of whether or not better prepared or more efficient candidates are found on the list. Even the question of priority of time placement on an eligible list should not be a determining factor in the selection of teachers. Eligible lists should be so merged that the best qualified candidates can be available when needed.

USE OF ELIGIBLE LISTS

In all the large city systems which require written examinations as part of their program of teacher selection, eligible lists are used

[1] Criterion II, p. 13.
[2] Criterion XVII, p. 23.

and have been found most practicable and successful. Either required by law or established by the board of education, these lists are prepared in order that only those who are qualified are available for assignment, and that such assignment can be based on merit. Eligible lists are also used in a few of the cities in listing normal school graduates who are eligible for appointment to elementary school positions without examinations. Several other cities, including Cincinnati, Oakland, and Milwaukee, use what is termed a "preferred list" or "ranking list" in determining those candidates who, after a review of their qualifications and experience, have demonstrated their fitness through a personal interview conducted by a special committee. No matter what the local conditions may be, the preparation of some type of eligible list is found practicable. Descriptions of various types of such lists and their operation are submitted from several cities.

In Philadelphia, as required by law, eligible lists, properly classified, containing the names of persons who have received certificates of qualification to teach, and arranged as nearly as possible in the order of rank or standing, must be kept in the office of the superintendent and open to inspection by members of the board of education, associate and district superintendents, principals, and school visitors. Furthermore, no teacher can be appointed or transferred to any educational position in the school system whose name does not appear among the three highest names on the proper eligible list. To carry out the provisions of the law, the board of education has established three practices:

1. Proper eligible lists are prepared and the classifications extended so that practically all positions coming under the Department of Superintendence are filled from such appropriate eligible lists.

2. The applicant whose name is first on the list is offered the first appointment; the second eligible the second appointment, and so on down the eligible list in order of rank or standing.

3. The names of unappointed applicants are retained on the eligible lists for a period of three years subject only to the provision that should the qualifying requirements be revised in any way by the board of education, the names of only those who meet the revised requirements are retained on the eligible lists.

In Boston the eligible lists of candidates with their respective ratings are annually established by the Board of Superintendence. The names of candidates who successfully pass the competitive examinations and obtain teaching certificates are arranged in graded eligible lists in the order of their respective qualifications as determined. No person may be appointed to a permanent position as a teacher whose name does not head the proper eligible list, provided that

> . . . if in the opinion of the Superintendent there is good reason why such person should not be appointed, he shall so certify to the School Committee, whereupon the regular procedure shall be followed with respect to the second person on the list; but the person appointed shall be one of the first three on said list willing to accept such appointment. The name of any person who has failed of appointment on three separate occasions when another person on the list has been selected shall be removed therefrom and shall not be restored thereto except by another examination.

In Los Angeles an "Eligible List" is used which contains the names of those applicants who have complied with all requirements and who have received in the competitive examination a grade of 85 per cent or more. The ranking on the eligible list is determined by the general average of all grades received by the applicant. The names of those eligibles who receive a grade of 85 per cent and less than 91 per cent remain on the eligible list for one year. The names of those with grades of 91 per cent and less than 95 per cent are retained for two years, while those with a grade of 95 per cent or over are kept on the list for three years. The list is revised after each examination and the names are ranked in the order of their grades. Section 425 of the Rules and Regulations of the Los Angeles City Board of Education explains the method of selecting eligibles from the list as follows:

> All teachers entering the school system shall be elected and assigned from the eligible list as long as there are persons on that list who can perform the duties required. Elections and assignments of entering teachers shall in general be made in the order in which the names appear on the eligible lists; provided, however, that for the good of the service the Superintendent may recommend for election, and may assign, that teacher among the first ten on the list who can best perform the required service; and provided further that, in case it is urgent to appoint a man-teacher in

junior or senior high schools, the Superintendent may recommend for election, and may assign, the best qualified man-teacher selected from among the first twenty-five on the list.

In Pittsburgh the applicant must receive a composite rating of 80 points or above in order to be placed on the eligible list. The list is made up each year and any applicant whose name is placed thereon in any one year may retain his original ranking as a basis of re-classification for the following year. He may, however, in order to improve his ranking take a re-examination and elect which records of the written examinations shall be counted by the Board of Education. Initial appointments are made from the three highest names on the list. On the other hand, the name of any person who refuses three offers of an initial appointment is automatically dropped from the eligible list.

In the city of Washington the names of successful candidates are arranged in order of rank in merged lists, or in new lists if there are no old lists to merge. From these lists appointments are made in the order of rank as vacancies occur in the positions for which the candidates have qualified. In New York City, however, there is no merging of the eligible lists. The life of the list is three years and a candidate who is not appointed during the life of a list must, if he desires to apply again for a teacher's license, take the examination again in its entirety. Appointments are in general made in the order of standing on the eligible list. If two or more candidates obtain identical final ratings, their names are placed on the list in the order of the "dates of receipt of their applications."

In Baltimore the average attained in the written examination and the average attained in practice teaching have equal weight in determining the ranking on the eligible lists for elementary school positions. The sum of these two averages, divided by two, gives the rank of each successful candidate on the eligible lists. Lists are merged after each examination period but no candidate continues on the list for a period longer than three years from the date of listing.

In some cities eligible lists for teaching positions in elementary schools are prepared from normal school records. In St. Louis graduates of the teacher-training institution are assigned to teaching positions in the order of their class rank at graduation. Jersey City,

Atlanta, and New Orleans are using the same procedure in preparing such eligible lists. In the last city named, the regulation of the Board of Education reads as follows:

> In recommending applicants for vacancies in the elementary grades of the white schools, preference shall be given to the graduates of the Normal School. These graduates must be listed in the order of their percentages—the names of the graduates of each succeeding class being merged at once with any existing list. The applicants are to be recommended for appointment by the Superintendent in the order in which the names appear on the list.

In those cities which do not hold competitive examinations and do not have ranking lists of graduates, a "preferred list" or "ranking list" is prepared for each of the various grades, departments, and subjects from all the applications received and filed during a period of from one to three years. The selection of candidates for these lists is usually based on character, personality, training, years, and quality of teaching experience as measured by inspection of credentials and certificates, personal interview, and sometimes by demonstration of teaching. The applicants are rated separately by two or more members of a selecting committee and at a conference a final mark or rank is agreed upon. Oakland, California, has a committee of three—the superintendent and two assistant superintendents—each of whom rates the applicant separately. The committee as a whole studies the individual ratings and agrees upon a final rank for the preferred list. Vacancies during the year are filled from this list.

Time Limits of Eligible Lists

The length of time that a person's name may be continued on the eligible list differs considerably in the cities studied. Where written examinations are held, the general rule is to retain names of unappointed eligibles on lists for a period of three years. Where ranking lists of normal school graduates are used, again the practice runs to a three-year period for continuing the names on the list. However, where there are no examinations and where preferred or eligible lists are based on rating by individuals or committees, such lists usually operate for one year. Where names are retained for more than one year and new eligible lists become available, due to annual examinations or graduations from normal school, the overwhelming practice is to merge the new list with the old, rearranging the names in order of rank. The merged list has the decided advantage of permitting the selection of those candidates who stand highest. The outstanding exceptions to this practice are to be found in Buffalo, Rochester, and New York City, where one eligible list must be exhausted before assignments can be made for a newer list. The Education Law for the State of New York reads, "Eligible lists shall not be merged and one list shall be exhausted before nominations are made from a list of a subsequent date." Failure to merge the lists works decidedly against the system in two ways. It compels the system to employ those far down on the old list who have not the high qualifications of those ranking near the top of the new lists. Also, quite a few of those ranking at the top of the newer lists have found it impossible to wait until the old lists have been exhausted and have sought positions in other communities. Thus their services have been lost to the system. In January, 1937, when the Board of Education of New York City appointed 790 new teachers, it found that more than 1000 men and women on its eligible lists were unwilling to accept the appointment. These candidates had passed the examinations one to seven years ago, but by the time the opportunity to be appointed had arisen, they had found other positions. Some had secured other positions in the system and were satisfied. Others were teaching in other school systems, some had found employment in business, while others had married and were no longer interested in teaching.

Order of Assignment or Appointment from the List

The order of assignment or appointment from the eligible list is fairly uniform where such lists are the result of competitive examinations or graduation rankings. Such assignment or appointment is usually made in the order in which the name appears on the list. This procedure holds good even though the superintendent may be permitted by law or regulation to select one of the three highest names on the list. If the superintendent has good reasons why the highest ranking candidate should not be assigned or appointed, he should, and in practice usually does, so certify to the board of education or school committee.

Summary and Conclusions

The study of the practices in the largest cities, as well as the realization of the requirements of any selective system based upon merit, leads to the recommendation of certain definite practices which are in accord with accepted principles of school administration and in keeping with the general criteria:

1. Lists of eligible candidates who have satisfactorily met all the requirements for teaching positions should be a necessary part of every program for the selection of teachers.

2. The preparation of such eligible lists would be influenced solely by the desire to use the best possible professional methods and techniques in selecting the most efficient teachers from the supply of available candidates.

3. Names of successful candidates should be arranged in graded eligible lists in the order of their respective qualifications or merit.

4. Separate eligible lists should be prepared for the different types or classifications of teaching positions so that as far as possible all positions coming under the superintendent can be filled from such appropriate eligible lists.

5. Eligible lists should be made up each year or as occasion demands; and lists should be merged so that at all times the successful candidates with the best qualifications or the highest rankings shall appear at the top of their respective lists.

6. No candidate should continue on the eligible list for a period longer than three years from the original date of listing.

7. Assignment or appointment should in general be made in the order in which the names appear on the eligible list.

8. Whenever the facts justify such action, the superintendent should have the power to recommend that the candidate at the top of the eligible list be not assigned or appointed to a particular vacancy. This recommendation, with a detailed report of the facts, should be communicated to the board of education for final approval.

PROBATIONARY SERVICE

A probationary or trial period should be required of all candidates who are assigned or appointed to a teaching position.[3] Even though

[3] Criterion XVIII, p. 24.

the candidate has successfully met all the qualifying requirements and has passed, where required, all oral and written examinations with a rating which clearly justifies the assignment or appointment, final election, permanent appointment, or a continuing contract should not follow without a satisfactory probationary service. Decisions concerning the permanency of appointment or tenure are to be made only on the basis of careful, objective evidence. This probationary or trial teaching period allows a splendid opportunity to learn more about the teacher's ability and fitness on the "job" before assignment or appointment becomes final. No current plan for the selection of teachers is so perfect, or likely to be, that this trial period can be discarded. Teaching at its best is a very complicated process and involves many variables which cannot be measured by an interview, a written examination, a demonstration lesson, or a close scrutiny and evaluation of credentials. An actual day-by-day service in the teaching situation itself, with proper supervision and observation, coupled with sympathetic understanding and guidance will furnish more adequate evidence upon which to base final recommendations.

Practice in the Largest Cities

In all the cities studied there is one requirement which is applicable to all candidates. They must serve a probationary period of teaching before permanent assignment or appointments are received. This probationary or trial teaching period is required of all who succeed in meeting the qualifications for a teaching position, whether they are beginners or experienced teachers. To be assigned or appointed beyond this period, it is required that the teacher must not only be successful but give evidence of growth warranting the expectation of service commensurate with the increasing salary provided by the schedule. On the other hand, the probationary period may be terminated before the time elapses, if it is evident that satisfactory service is not being rendered by the teacher on probation.

Practice seems to be divided between one year as the probationary period and three years, with a slight majority in favor of the longer trial period. Even in those cities where the one-year period is the rule, such as Philadelphia, Baltimore, Detroit, Washington, the probationary period can be extended on recommendation of the super-intendent of schools, subject to the approval of the board of education. Appointment or assignment to which a graded salary is attached is for a probation period of one year. At the close of the one-year period the services of the teacher who is unsatisfactory are automatically discontinued unless an extension of the probation is granted. Usually the total probation in such cases cannot exceed two years.

In the cities where the three-year period of probation is required, such as Cleveland, Atlanta, New York, Minneapolis, Providence, Denver, New Orleans, the teacher is not assured, however, of three years of teaching. During the three-year period, annual assignment or appointment, with or without salary advancement at schedule rates, depends upon the recommendation of the superintendent, subject to the approval of the board of education. If at any time during the probation, or at the expiration thereof, the services of the teacher are found unsatisfactory, the probationary assignment may be terminated. One city (Los Angeles), setting two years as its probationary period, rules that after two full consecutive years of satisfactory service, probationary teachers shall be promoted to the regular staff and shall be classified as permanent teachers.

Summary and Conclusions

At best, the probationary period should be considered an adjustment period for the successful applicant in her own new teaching situation. Granted that the qualifications have been successfully met and that the preparation for the particular position has been adequate, the new teacher must go through a period of orientation and adjustment. Her greatest need at this time is not "inspection" or "evaluation," but sympathetic guidance and helpful suggestions from the supervisory agents available. In practice, however, this probationary period has been made a time for rigid supervisory visits, criticisms, and ratings. From an administrative standpoint the probationary period affords the opportunity for a quick dismissal, without "trial," for unsatisfactory service. A one-, two-, or three-year "on trial" period allows time to observe the teacher in a real classroom situation over an extended schedule of teaching assignments, to evaluate her teaching, and to estimate her ability to grow and develop and become an asset to the system before final election.

Yet the probationary period is not solely for the newly appointed teacher. Any teacher at any time, no matter how long she has been in the school system, can be on probation. This is a question of supervision and teacher rating. There is nothing to prevent the proper supervisory officers in any city system from rating a teacher unsatisfactory and putting that teacher on probation. Even where tenure laws apply, a teacher can be placed on probation and later dismissed from the service for good and sufficient cause. In Detroit, as an example, after a year of probationary service, the teacher is given a continuing contract for the following year and succeeding years. All teachers who have served less than one year and all teachers who are not rendering satisfactory service are classified as probationary teachers and their contracts are subject to cancellation by the board for cause upon thirty days' notice. Even regular teachers with years of service to their credit whose work is judged to be unsatisfactory are placed on the probationary list at the end of any semester. A teacher whose service is of doubtful merit may be continued as a probationary teacher a second year, but no teacher is given more than two years of trial as a probationary teacher.

The problem is not one solely associated with the initial employment of a teacher, unless it is acknowledged and accepted as a final "sieve" to eliminate the mistakes made through the operation of teacher-selection procedures. Nor is the probationary period a device to impress upon the newly appointed teacher the fact that she is on trial for a certain length of time. That goes without saying. However, it should be the recognized and accepted period for helpful and sympathetic guidance and stimulating supervisory activities on the part of the supervisors and the supervising principals. A reasonable degree of security conditioned on satisfactory service and professional improvement is the right of every teacher, either newly appointed or long in service.

CHAPTER X

RECRUITING STUDENTS FOR TEACHER TRAINING

THE OBLIGATION OF SELECTING AGENCIES FOR THE RECRUITMENT OF STUDENTS FOR TEACHER TRAINING

ANY program of teacher selection which has for its goal the securing of well-trained teachers must, of necessity, be a very comprehensive one, requiring high standards of performance at every step in the preparation for the profession. The most important step in this preparation is the selective admission or recruitment for teacher training.[1] It is here that every possible method should be employed in selecting the most promising and in eliminating the inferior student. For a long while the important consideration was given to the number of years of normal or teachers college training necessary to fulfill the requirements, regardless of the fitness of the student. Moreover, until very recently, the requirement of four years of high school work prerequisite to entrance was practically the only uniform procedure in the process of pre-training selection.[2] Superintendents of cities in or near which tax-supported teacher-training institutions are located have the opportunity as well as the responsibility to cooperate in providing an adequate supply of well-educated, adequately trained, and thoroughly competent recruits. They can establish more or less extensive technics for pre-training selection and refuse admission to their municipal or state institutions, or withhold approval or certification for admission to private institutions. On the other hand, if the teacher's influence upon the lives of children is as important as educators claim, it would seem that common prudence would require that teacher-training institutions admit, for the teaching profession, only the most intelligent and those most promising in character and personality. There is this joint responsibility of the public school system and the teacher-

[1] Criterion XIX, p. 24.
[2] Cooke, Dennis H., *Problems of the Teaching Personnel*, p. 26.

training institution for the competence, through careful and wise selection of recruits, of the teaching staff.

A POLICY OF SELECTIVE ADMISSION TO TEACHER-TRAINING INSTITUTIONS

Admission to any teacher-training institution should be considered a privilege and not a right. Accordingly, admission should be granted only to those who are qualified. The superintendent and those associated with him in teacher selection are compelled to consider their own high school graduates. It is at this point that a policy of selective admission should begin. Certainly mere graduation from an accredited high school is not to be the only factor in determining entrance to the institutions preparing teachers. As many factors or measures of abilities and traits as can be made available should be used as a basis in determining fitness for such admission.

If instead of that one measure (high-school graduation), the institutions required a record of courses taken and grades made in both elementary and high schools, certificates from the high-school principal concerning character and personality traits suitable for teachers, a complete health examination, a general ability examination and some achievement tests in pivotal subjects given at the institution, a personal interview, and a declaration of desire and intention to teach, it has been shown that a student's probable success in the institution and as a teacher can be foretold with much more accuracy than is possible when only one or two such measures are used.[3]

Cooke believes that "pre-training selection can be done in the most effective manner on the basis of intelligence tests, achievement tests and achievement in high school subjects, moral and social characteristics, personality ratings, recommendations of the high school principal and superintendent, aptitude tests, and reports of guidance officials, if such are available."[4] In general, a policy of selective admission would consider such qualifications as high scholarship, capacity for mental growth, healthy body free from major physical defects which would render the student unfit for teaching, good speech, high moral character as indicated in the personal life

[3] National Survey of the Education of Teachers, Vol. VI: *Summary and Interpretations*, p. 146. 1935.

[4] Cooke, Dennis H., *op. cit.*, p. 34.

of the student, interest in and enthusiasm for teaching, and emotional fitness. Superintendents and state departments have established definite policies regarding admission to teacher-training institutions. While these policies differ as to standards and types of qualifications to be met, there is evident in all of them a desire to work out an effective program of recruit selection.

CONTINUATION OF THE POLICY OF SELECTION AND ELIMINATION THROUGHOUT THE ENTIRE TRAINING PERIOD

The responsibility of the teacher-training institutions in the program of selective admission does not cease when the successful high school graduate has been admitted. Since no selecting devices or measures are absolutely reliable, and since it is quite true that doubtful recruits may have been admitted for training, a rigid policy of selection and elimination must continue throughout the training period. Such institutions must continue to guide, direct, and approve the student's growth as a potential teacher and his fitness for the teaching profession. Skillful direction, wise supervision, and courageous elimination must go on in order to insure well-trained prospective teachers.

Accordingly, at stated intervals or at logical places in the teacher-training curricula, the teaching and the supervisory staffs should raise the question of the fitness of each student to continue his special training. This continuous program of checking and guidance will provide for elimination of those unfit or lacking in those qualities and traits which are considered essential in the teaching profession. However, it is only fair to state that such elimination should carry with it the responsibility of directing the eliminated student into other types of work for which he is best fitted.

Practices in Recruitment for Teacher Training

A considerable number of the larger cities have definitely planned a program of recruitment for teacher training on a selective basis. For example, Philadelphia has established the following regulations:

Bona fide residents who are graduated from a public high school shall, upon recommendation of the principal of the high school, be eligible for admission to the Normal School under the following conditions:

a. That their credentials from the high school shall show that they have accomplished the minimum requirements for Normal School entrance in the subjects prescribed by action of the Committee on Schools of the Board.

b. That they shall have received a general average of at least 80 at graduation and also an average of not less than 75 for the work done in English in the final year in which this subject was taken.

c. That they shall have passed satisfactorily a physical examination conducted by the Division of Medical Inspection.

d. That they shall have passed satisfactorily a personality examination conducted under the direction of the Superintendent of Schools.

e. That their admission shall be for a probationary period not to exceed one year, during which time, on recommendation of the principal of the Normal School and approval of the Superintendent of Schools, the names of students who have shown themselves unqualified by reason of temperament, personality, or other cause, for the profession of teaching shall be dropped from the roll of the school.

Bona fide residents of the city who are graduated from institutions other than the public high schools giving courses equivalent to those required for graduation from the public high schools, and meeting the entrance requirements shall be eligible to take an examination for admission to the Normal School. Such examination shall be conducted under the direction of the Superintendent of Schools, and a general average of 80 with a minimum of 75 in English, shall be required as the passing mark.

Another city (Baltimore) is meeting the problem of recruitment for teacher training through the following admission requirements:

Graduates of the secondary schools who are recommended by the several faculties as having the personal qualities desirable in teachers of the young may offer their averages in making application for admission to a Normal School or Teacher Training School.

It is recommended that the principals of the senior high schools be instructed to recommend no graduate for admission to a normal school or teacher training school unless the graduate shall have attained an average in scholarship of at least 80 per cent, this average to be based on the work in major subjects done in the last two years of high school.

Preference shall be given to those whose scholarship average for the last two years is highest.

An opportunity for application, limited to a date named, shall be given before the admission of a new class, and the names of those applying shall be placed in the order of averages among the names already on the list before the admissions are made.

All graduates of the Senior High Schools who are eligible for entrance into the Normal School must be examined prior to their entrance and

1. Those with remediable (physical) defects must have same corrected before admission.
2. Those with irremediable (physical) defects will be notified that they cannot be recommended for admission to the Normal Schools.

No candidate shall be enrolled in a normal school or teacher training school who has not reached the age of sixteen years before the thirty-first of December of the same year.

In one of the southern cities (Atlanta), the superintendent has had his board of education adopt the following rules governing admission to the normal school:

Graduates from high schools having an approved four-year course are admitted to the Normal Training School, without examination within three years after graduation, upon the recommendation of the principal of the high school.

Applicants not presenting diplomas from fully accredited high schools, or institutions of equal rank, must pass examinations on the subjects included in a four-year high school course.

All applicants must be of a pleasing appearance and be physically, mentally, and morally fit to undertake the responsibilities of the profession of teaching.

The number of students to be admitted in this school shall be determined by the Superintendent, subject to the approval of the Board.

More recently adopted regulations regarding recruitment for teacher training in another southern city (New Orleans) indicate a definite attempt to meet this important problem. These regulations include the following:

Applicants for admission to the Normal School must be graduates of a high school of recognized standing and must be eligible for entrance to standard colleges as candidates for the Bachelor degree, and in addition must have made a general average of 85 per cent with a minimum grade of 85 per cent in English.

Applicants for admission to the Normal School who are graduates of high schools but have not met the conditions named above, must evidence in a written examination conducted by the faculty of the Normal School in the week preceding the opening of the term, that they have the knowledge equivalent to the courses prescribed for entrance to the Normal School, by making an average grade of 85 per cent in all subjects with a minimum of 85 per cent in English and of 70 per cent in each of the other subjects.

All applicants for admission to the Normal School must obtain from the Medical Director a certificate of health and physical soundness. No applicant will be admitted until said certificate shall have been filed with the Principal. Applicants exhibiting physical defects of any nature shall be notified that unless such defects are corrected within the first three months' attendance in the Normal School, they will be excluded from the school.

The function of the Normal School being the education and training of teachers, no student shall be permitted to retain his connection with that school who is unsatisfactory in deportment or scholarship.

Another city included in this study (Cleveland) is trying to select competent recruits for the Junior Teachers' College or Normal Department through the following regulations adopted by the Board of Education of the City School District:

Applicants presenting credentials of graduation from an approved (membership in the North Central Association or its equivalent) secondary school or equivalent may be admitted providing the applicant presents

1. An official statement indicating that she ranked in the upper half of her class in scholarship.
2. A statement signed by the principal indicating that in his judgment the applicant ranked in the upper half of her class in personal fitness for the teaching profession.

Applicants not qualified for admission under the above may be admitted on examination—the extent, nature, time, etc., of such examination being determined by the dean of the School of Education, with the approval of the superintendent of schools.

Each applicant, before admission, shall be required to present a satisfactory medical certificate from the school physician recommending her for entrance into the school. In the granting of such medical certificates, the school physician is expected to adhere to the same standards as obtain in the granting of health certificates for regular teaching appointments in the city public schools.

After formal admission of the applicant, the dean of the School of Education shall, when so recommended by three-fourths vote of the faculty, advise any student to withdraw from the school, who in the judgment of the faculty is below the standard of scholarship or personal fitness required for teaching service in the city public schools.

All regulations in reference to the conduct of courses, changes in courses, scholarship requirements, residence requirements, advanced standing, promotion, attendance, discipline, student life and organizations, etc., shall be left to the jurisdiction of the dean of the School of Education, subject to the approval of the superintendent of schools, with the understanding that the retention in the school, the promotion, and the graduation of any student shall depend upon her record as to personal fitness for the teaching profession no less than upon her excellence in scholarship and success in practice teaching.

In the administration of the above regulations, neither the superintendent of schools nor the administrative officers of the School of Education are authorized to make any exception without the formal approval of the board of education.

On the other hand, state departments of education, issuing state teachers' certificates which are recognized in many of the cities considered in this study, have effectively cooperated with superintendents and boards of education in raising the standards for the admission of students to study and practice the teaching profession in state normal schools and teachers colleges. The most recent changes were made by the Board of Regents of the State Department of Education, New York, at its regular meeting held July 29, 1935, when the following admission regulations were adopted:

1. *Merit and fitness.* The sole basis for granting an applicant admission to a state normal school or state college for teachers shall be apparent merit and fitness to perform the duties usually required of students preparing for admission to practice the profession of teaching. In determining the fitness of applicants, the state normal school or college for teachers shall employ examinations, conduct personal interviews, and make investigations covering any or all of the following qualifications, abilities, or traits:

   a. Moral character as indicated in the personal life of the applicant, in the record of the applicant as a high school student, and in his record as a participant in the examinations conducted by representatives of the state teacher training institutions.

   b. Physical fitness for teaching, personal appearance and bearing.

   c. Quality and use of voice, correct use and command of language, both in writing and in speech.

   d. General intelligence, culture and scholarship.

   e. Personal and social attributes and power to win and hold the respect and cooperation of fellow students and teachers.

f. Technical skill in a special subject such as music, art, commerce, industrial arts, homemaking, etc., in case of an applicant desiring to enroll in such specialized department.

g. Interest in and enthusiasm for teaching.

2. *Kinds of examinations and interviews.* The means to be employed in the inquiry as to the several items of the above schedule shall be one or more of the following:

a. Written examinations.

b. Formal interviews.

c. Practical tests of technical ability.

d. General physical examinations conducted by authorized physicians.

e. Speech examinations conducted by qualified representatives of state teacher educating institutions.

f. Informal interviews, correspondence, and investigations otherwise conducted.

3. *Scope of examinations.* The various forms of examinations to be employed, the general scope of the examination, and the tests to be included under it as well as the relative rates of the various parts of the examination shall be determined by the state committee on selective admission, subject to the approval of the Commissioner of Education, in advance of the examination itself.

4. *Eligibility for admission to examination.* Competitive examinations shall be open to a high school senior or a high school graduate who will complete or has completed the requirements for a state high school diploma or approved equivalent preparation, who maintained during his high school course a standard of scholarship satisfactory to the Commissioner of Education, who is or will be at least sixteen years of age at date of entrance to the state normal school or state college for teachers, who is a citizen of the United States, and who intends to teach in the public schools of the State of New York for a period of not less than two years subsequent to the completion of a professional curriculum.[5]

Summary and Conclusions

Recruitment for teacher training is undoubtedly recognized as one of the steps in any program of teacher selection.[6] Consequently, the agency or organization set up by the superintendent of schools and his board of education should include it as one of its important func-

[5] Cooper, Herman, "Report on Admission Regulations." *New York State Education,* December, 1935, p. 232.

[6] Criterion XIX, p. 24.

tions, especially where a tax-supported teachers college or normal school is established as part of the municipal school system or is set up within the state for its benefit. This function of recruitment for teacher training becomes the agency's first opportunity to establish such measures as will prove most effective in selecting prospective teachers, not only that the product of the teacher-training institution will be of a high order, but also that the tax-paying community will not be wasteful in spending money upon candidates for teaching who are not likely to be very successful.

From an analysis of the regulations concerning admissions to teacher-training institutions operating in the cities studied, the following requirements are most frequently set forth:

1. Graduation from an approved high school or its equivalent.
2. Satisfactory completion of an approved or prescribed high school course, or its equivalent satisfied by examination.
3. A scholastic ranking of approximately 80 per cent (general average) with no grade in any subject below 70 per cent.
4. An average of 80 per cent or better in English.
5. A physical examination under the supervision of the board of education, which provides for the immediate elimination of those with irremediable defects.
6. An age requirement of at least 16 years at the time of entrance to the teacher-training institution.
7. Citizenship.
8. A recommendation from the principal of the high school.
9. A personality report.
10. Provisions for dropping from the teacher-training institution those who show themselves unqualified by reason of temperament, personality, scholarship, or conduct or such cause as makes them unsatisfactory as teachers.

The first four requirements are deemed necessary since they offer valuable evidence concerning certain essential qualifications for teacher training. These are: (*a*) the mental ability to complete successfully an approved four-year high school course; (*b*) a fairly complete mastery of the elementary school subject matter; (*c*) a preparation which insures a fair amount of general and cultural training. Moreover, the high academic standing will indicate what seriousness the applicant takes to his teacher training. The chances are he will apply the same energy to his new studies and opportunities.

Both the recommendation of the high school principal and personality report (Requirements 8 and 9) are factors to be seriously considered in the admission of high school graduates to teacher-training institutions. The first of these carries with it the certification by the authority of the school that the individual applicant has satisfied the scholastic requirements; that the records are authentic; that, as far as the school has the information, the applicant is of high moral character; and that the applicant is a desirable recruit for the teaching profession. The personality report, which varies from a single rating (superior, good, or undesirable) to a rather elaborate case study, can become an important factor, especially when the study is based on reports from many sources dealing with the personal and social attributes as indicated in the life of the applicant in as well as out of school. These reports will be the results of personal interviews, classroom, home, and social contacts over a period of time, guidance programs, character and personality testimonials, psychological tests, and the study of extracurricular activities and interests. Such information can be of great importance in selecting recruits with those personality traits which are considered highly desirable and perhaps essential to teaching success, but which they believe cannot, as yet, be measured properly by any written examination. While no one list of such personality elements is standard, the following items include those which are most frequently mentioned:

1. Personal habits; habitual neatness; cleanliness; orderliness.
2. Promptness and regularity.
3. Habitual refinement, good manners, tact, courtesy, unselfishness, self-control.
4. Habitual industry, reliability, enthusiasm, honesty, integrity.
5. Habitual kindliness, cheerfulness, sympathy.
6. Loyalty to the school, to organized society; the spirit of service and cooperation.
7. General influence for good.

In a few cases these reports have included the results of intelligence and psychological tests which are significant for predicting academic success.

These requirements are to be commended and should be included in every program dealing with recruitment for teacher training. To carry them out successfully becomes a fourfold problem, involving

1. School superintendents and their organized agencies for teacher selection.
2. Guidance counselors and their programs for proper vocational guidance.
3. Teacher-training institutions and their program of cooperation with the public school administrators.
4. Educators and psychologists working together in research, analyzing teaching aptitude and fitness, and devising better means of measuring or recognizing it.

In most of the cities studied where the municipal school system includes teacher-training facilities, the agencies established for teacher selection are endeavoring to bring about the close cooperation of these four groups. To insist upon this working together and to plan for it is of first importance. Where the public school systems do not have their own facilities for teacher training, the responsibility must rest with the state education department.

> The most important of all state educational functions are the selection, training, and development of its teachers. No state can carry forward an effective program of education if the teacher-training facilities for teachers in any field of public education, kindergarten, elementary, secondary, or evening school, whether in academic, vocational, or supervisory lines, are controlled, in whole or in part, by an association of private colleges, or by any other agency except the office which has control and supervision of the public schools of the state. No state can assign this task. It cannot sublet. It cannot ignore. It must merely control. It must organize and control.[7]

Even in these cities the superintendent of schools can use his influence to have the state department of education choose with care those whom the state admits to its teacher-training institutions. This influence will be most effective if the school authorities include in their programs the following procedures:

[7] National Education Association, *Twelfth Yearbook of the Department of Superintendence*, p. 126.

1. Make definite recommendations from time to time concerning proper standards for admission to the teacher-training institutions. These recommendations must consider the growth of the local community, changes in its social and economic life, and the changes and expansion of the educational offerings.

2. Secure through the state department of education proper inspection and rating of all private teacher-training institutions of the state.

3. Build up within the local system an adequate guidance program which will encourage promising high school graduates to prepare for admission to teaching, and will likewise discourage those who are not likely to succeed in the profession.

4. Cooperate with all teacher-training institutions wherever feasible, by providing opportunities in their local system for observation and practice teaching for students in training.

5. Encourage, where facilities are available, cooperative programs of educational experiments with the teacher-training institutions. "The fact that experimentation is going on and that the city school staff and the staff of the institution from which the city recruits its teachers are engaged in educational research is one of the surest ways of making certain that the teacher training institution is kept keenly aware of the problems to be met by its graduates." [8]

On the other hand, all teacher-training institutions must remain in constant touch with local school systems, be continually alive to their constant changes and ever-growing demands. All administrative barriers and differences in educational policies and philosophies should be subordinated and all the splendid opportunities for teacher preparation should be utilized on an intimate and professional basis of cooperation.

The institutions in any State which have been approved for the education of teachers should cooperate in developing and enforcing a program of increasingly rigorous selective admission of students to curricula for teachers. Such a program should include the use of as many measures of personality, scholarship aptitude, health, and general ability as possible. Until an easily administered, valid, and reliable predictive test of general

[8] Evenden, E. S., "The Superintendent of Schools and the Education of Teachers," p. 208.

ability is devised, the use of several measures will provide a better basis for selection than dependence upon high school grades, position in the graduating class, or similar measures.[9]

Thus both the public schools and the teacher-training institutions must realize that teaching is a privilege and not a right, and so work together in adopting a policy and formulating a program of selective admission or recommendation to such institutions, basing selection on the best and most reliable criteria, continuously corrected; and continue to cooperate in guiding, directing, and appraising the growth of these recruits as potential teachers.

[9] National Survey of the Education of Teachers, Vol. II, *Teacher Personnel in the United States*, p. 107.

PART III

General Summary and Recommendations

CHAPTER XI

GENERAL SUMMARY AND RECOMMENDATIONS

THIS study endeavors to present a comprehensive survey of the administrative practices in the largest cities in the field of teacher selection, project these practices in the light of basic criteria, and recommend standards for the organization and administration of this important function. The foregoing chapters deal primarily with the various procedures and methods used by school authorities, and include detailed findings of the survey organized according to the different aspects of the problem. Each chapter contains its own summary and conclusions.

It must be kept in mind, however, that no attempt has been made to evaluate the complete program of teacher selection in any city or to rank the cities included in the survey on the basis of the criteria. There is no one city program of teacher selection that is perfect or wholly ideal and none that is wholly bad. Some have made a consistently better showing in meeting the basic criteria proposed than have others. There is none but that has its peaks and its valleys in conformance with the recommended standards which are in keeping with the criteria and sound school administration. On the other hand, the study investigates each step or procedure in the complete program of teacher selection, compares practices in the various cities, and summarizes the findings. From these recommendations are made and standards are proposed which are supported by the weight of practice and educational authorities and which are in keeping with the basic criteria listed in Chapter II. This concluding chapter aims to review, briefly, the major recommendations in each of the eight major divisions in a program of teacher selection.

ORGANIZING AND ADMINISTERING THE PROGRAM
OF TEACHER SELECTION

The selection of teachers is an administrative function for which the superintendent of schools should be held responsible. The responsibility, which is a most important one, carries with it two outstanding obligations: to secure the best trained teachers that can be secured under the prevalent salary schedule; and to base the program of teacher selection upon merit. The techniques employed in the selection of teachers will be in keeping with the democratic principle of equality of opportunity in accordance with merit. No appointment will be made for political purposes, or on the basis of personal friendship, family relationship, religious affiliation, or other non-professional reasons. There will be no attempt to find positions for individuals, but a carefully planned endeavor will be made to find qualified and efficient candidates to fill particular positions. Such conditions are necessary in order that all appointments may be made on the basis of merit, a requirement of an effective personnel system.

The actual work of administering the program of teacher selection should be delegated to a competent official with an adequate organization or assisting staff, under the direction of the superintendent. The selecting agency, thus organized, should be composed of those best qualified, should have access to expert opinion and assistance of specialists, should be free from all non-educational and non-professional influences, and should operate effectively in the selection of the best-equipped and in the elimination of the unfit and undesirable candidates for the teaching positions. Effective personnel administration requires men and women with adequate training for the work they are to perform and with qualities of character adequate for the positions they are to occupy. The best procedures that may be established for the selection of teachers may be virtually annulled if they are administered by an incapable or unsympathetic staff.

RECRUITING THE CANDIDATES

Wherever possible, selecting agencies should seek desirable candidates for the teaching positions. They should not wait passively for applicants to apply. Recruitment should be active. Well-qualified persons are to be sought out and urged to apply. As many sources of supply as are available should be explored. It is held that the two best sources for such candidates are other school systems and the teacher-training institutions. Cooperative arrangement for the recommendation and certification of candidates can be and should be developed with accredited educational institutions which train for teaching. Moreover, no program of recruiting candidates should depend either upon the chance receipt of applications or upon its own local supply. Nor should the agency select a preponderance of any teaching staff from a small number of institutions. An excessive or harmful in-breeding should be avoided. On the other hand, candidates should be selected for specific positions which may demand special qualifications. Selecting agencies should make available definite information covering not only general and special qualifications for the various teaching positions but also the necessary procedures to be followed in applying. Such circulars of information should be so worded and arranged that they are readily comprehended.

Complete reliable information concerning the qualifications of all candidates should be secured. This information should be obtained through reliable sources and by uniform practices which cannot be criticized because of unfairness, incompleteness, or lack of proper certification or verification. The information should be secured from three sources: the candidate himself; from the candidate's references; and from other competent referees acting for the selecting agency. The use of a well-planned application blank is urged as a uniform method to obtain definite information concerning the candidate; but such information should be purely objective, readily determined or verified, and of the type that will determine his eligibility.

Reference reports or letters of recommendation should be secured from those competent persons who are best acquainted with the candidate and his work. Besides the various items dealing with the necessary or desirable traits and qualities set up by the selecting agency, the reference report should provide for suitable definitions and explanations of terms as well as a definite plan for checking or rating. Best practice seems to indicate a five-point scale for rating. To be used only in a confidential and professional manner, the reference report should be studied to verify the general qualifications of the candidate and to ascertain his weaknesses or undesirable qualities. It is recommended that at least three reference reports should be secured for each candidate, and that these reports should be used in connection with the personal interview. Reference reports should be rated according to a planned rating scale.

Thus far, the information about any candidate has been obtained through written and documentary sources. Those who are eligible for further consideration should now be interviewed by members or designated agents of the selecting staff. If possible, a personal interview should be held with every candidate who has satisfactorily met the minimum or desirable qualifications for the position. It is recommended that at least three interviewers individually meet the candidate. A well-planned check list with a rating sheet providing for separate ratings on specific items and for a general rating should be established by the selecting agency and used by each interviewer. Practice again favors a five-point rating scale.

Moreover, every candidate should be required to demonstrate his teaching ability in the classroom. If possible, he should be observed in his own teaching situation; otherwise, in the system where he is seeking appointment. No matter what may be the qualifications and rating of the candidate, he should not be considered for a teaching position if he does not show teaching ability which meets the approved standards set by the selecting agency. Designated agents and supervisory officers in other school systems and in teacher-training institutions can be called upon to make this required procedure possible and effective.

In addition, a physical or medical examination based on approved standards should be required of every candidate who has otherwise satisfactorily met all requirements. This examination should be given by competent examiners approved by the medical profession and under the direction of the selecting agency. The examining physicians should be responsible to the superintendent and their definite recommendations should be made to that executive. As the result of the physical or medical examination, candidates should be classified into three groups: those found free of physical defects and meeting the health standards; those with remediable defects which may have prejudicial influences on the efficiency of teaching; and those with irremediable defects. Those in the second group may be granted provisional assignment only, pending satisfactory treatment, with a definite time limit and a subsequent examination required. Those in the third group should be rejected. To avoid useless applications and examinations and to encourage more effective guidance during the training period, the health and physical standards should be made available to every prospective candidate; and publicity should be given to these standards in the teacher-training institutions.

USING THE WRITTEN EXAMINATION IN TEACHER SELECTION

It is held that written examinations are not necessary either to establish a basis for a list of eligibles in a program of teacher selection or to issue teacher licenses or certifications. Moreover, they do not test the teaching qualities of the candidate. On the other hand, the careful examination and interpretation of high school, college, and university records can measure the candidate's proficiency in his major and minor fields of specialization. If written examinations are to be given as a necessary procedure in a program of teacher selection, they could well be confined to those seeking positions for which no special training is now being given in standard colleges and universities. Subject matter examinations would then be limited to those subjects definitely related to such special positions. If local conditions demand some type of written examination, the examination could well be confined to a professional test for teachers. It is held that better understanding and cooperation between teacher-training institutions and selecting agencies will tend to eliminate all written examinations. The trend clearly indicates an increasing recognition and value given to certified evidence of academic and professional preparation made in accredited institutions. Moreover, the development and enforcement of a more professional program for the selection and admission of students for teacher training will do much to eliminate any need for the written examination. Proper certification and better practice teaching standards will also make unnecessary any technical examinations or demonstrations of personal skill. This also applies to special examinations in English, speech, or handwriting.

ESTABLISHING MINIMUM QUALIFICATIONS FOR TEACHING

As a necessary procedure in a program of teacher selection, minimum qualifications should be established for every type of teaching position. The first of these, minimum training requirements, should include general academic training, specific training in the special field, and professional training. It is desirable that the minimum requirement be four years of college preparation for the elementary teacher and five years for the secondary teacher. However, it is hoped that the near future will see this minimum upgraded to four years of general collegiate study followed by a two- or three-year period of strictly professional preparation at the graduate level. It should be kept in mind that mere increase in the time requirement or even the listing of additional prescribed courses will not of itself raise the professional standards of candidates. Time spent in college classrooms or elsewhere is certainly not a reliable index of intelligence, culture, personality, or other professionally desirable qualities. If teacher-training institutions admit students of non-professional caliber and low intelligence and are lax in their guidance and elimination during the training period, the upgrading of minimum requirements may prove of little avail and not notably raise professional standards.

Age requirements, while reflecting administrative policies and local conditions, are established to prohibit the initial appointment of relatively young teachers and to discourage the applications of those who may offer little or no hope for further professional growth. The minimum requirement of four years of college preparation will set, for the most part, the lower age limit. Administrative practices tend to set the upper age limit at forty or forty-five. Fitness for the particular position should always be the deciding factor; and even if local conditions have established age limits, exceptions should be permitted under proper regulation, upon the recommendation of the superintendent, followed by open discussion and approval by the board of education.

Previous teaching experience cannot be and need not be required of every candidate in every program of teacher selection.

The question of the marital status of a candidate should not be a factor in teacher selection.

VERIFYING AND EVALUATING THE CANDIDATE'S CREDENTIALS

Careful examination and verification of all credentials and records of the candidate are necessary in every program of teacher selection.

Documentary evidence can and should be obtained to support the following types of credentials: specific training in the special field; professional training in the field of Education; general training; general academic studies; scholarship record; confidential or reference reports concerning personality, ability, and success as a teacher; experience (if required); and age. All credentials should be from accredited or approved sources. They should first be checked to ascertain whether the candidate has satisfied the minimum requirements set up by the selecting agency. The credentials of those candidates who have met the requirements should then be studied and evaluated in order to determine the superior qualifications of any one candidate as compared with the qualifications of all the others applying for the same position. It is recommended that the selecting agency establish some uniform method for evaluating and an acceptable scale for rating such credentials. This grading or rating plan should allow for additional acceptable training and preparation beyond the minimum requirements. Certain maximum credit limits should be fixed, however, which should be based on a study of the teaching personnel in the system, the principle of diminishing returns, and any local situations which might condition them. The plan should also recognize the qualitative differences in the training of candidates as shown by scholastic ratings or averages made in accredited institutions. The rating of the credentials resulting from a carefully planned evaluation should play an important part in the final rating.

ASSIGNING OR APPOINTING THE CANDIDATE

In order that all assignments or appointments may be made on the basis of merit, all candidates who have satisfactorily met the necessary requirements should be listed under the proper classifications and in order of rank or standing. The final general rating of the candidate, based on the separate ratings assigned to his complete credentials, the personal interview, and the observed teaching, should be used in placing the candidate's name on the eligible list. Should any other factor be required by the local situation, such as a written examination, that rating should also be used in determining the final general rating. It is recommended that eligible lists be established each year, or as occasion demands, and be merged, so that at all times those with the best qualifications and the highest general ratings shall appear at the top of the list. No candidate should be continued on the eligible list longer than three years. At the same time it should be made known to all candidates that placement on an eligible list does not guarantee assignment or appointment. It does notify the candidate that he is eligible to consideration for assignment in comparison to all others on the list. These eligible lists should be open to the public. Priority of time placement on an eligible list should not be a factor in assigning teachers from the list. In general, assignment or appointment should be made in the order in which the names appear on the list. If a particular situation demands a departure from this general rule, the superintendent should have the right, within certain limits, to so recommend to the board of education for its approval.

After assignment or appointment, a probationary or trial period should be required of all candidates before final election. While practice varies, it is held that no one should be required to serve more than two years as a probationary teacher. It is quite conceivable, however, that the probationary period may vary and that the superintendent may be ready to recommend for final election at any time during the two-year period. With a highly successful teacher brought into the system from another city, a few months' trial period might suffice. This probationary period should be a period for helpful and sympathetic guidance and stimulating supervisory activities. However, in too many of the cities studied this period is without significance. It should be a time of positive demonstration of fitness for further employment. Once a teacher has acquired a kind of equity in the position, removal is often very difficult. Moreover, it is grossly unfair to the teacher, since he becomes more removed from alternative opportunities the longer he is retained. During the probationary period service records should be kept and at stated intervals reports can be made by the supervisory officers. At the end of the period a definite recommendation should be required with reference to the future appointment and placement of the probationer.

RECRUITING STUDENTS FOR TEACHER TRAINING

The most important step in the program of teacher selection is the selective admission or recruitment of students for teacher training.

Superintendents and their selecting agencies have the responsibility and the opportunity to cooperate in providing an adequate supply of well-educated, adequately trained and thoroughly competent recruits. They should establish techniques for pre-training selection and should refuse admission to municipal and state institutions or withhold approval or certification for admission to private institutions of high school graduates who are not capable or promising in character and personality.

Admission to any teacher-training institution should be considered a privilege and not a right. A policy of selective admission should be carefully planned and rigidly enforced. Fitness for such admission should be based on as many factors or measures of abilities and traits as can be made available. They should consider high scholarship, capacity for mental growth, healthy body free from major physical defects, good speech, high moral character as indicated in the personal life of the student, interest in and enthusiasm for teaching, and emotional fitness. Measures of these abilities and traits are to be obtained through intelligence and achievement tests, school records, personality ratings, recommendations of principal and teachers, physical examinations, and reports of guidance officials.

The policy of selective admission should be continued throughout the training period. Through proper supervision, the training institution must continue to guide, direct, and approve the student's growth as a potential teacher and his fitness for the teaching profession. This program of checking and guidance will demand courageous elimination of the unfit throughout the training period.

Boards of education, superintendents, selecting agencies, high school faculties on the one hand, and teacher-training institutions and supervisory agencies on the other, must cooperate in developing and enforcing an acceptable program of increasing rigorous selective admission to teacher-training institutions. All administrative barriers should be subordinated so that all the opportunities for student recruitment, teacher preparation, and teacher selection can be utilized on an effective professional basis.

PART IV

Bibliography

BIBLIOGRAPHY

Annual Reports of City School Systems.

ALMACK, J. C. "Selection of Teachers." *American School Board Journal*, November, 1920.

ALMACK, J. C. AND LANG, A. R. *Problems of the Teaching Profession.* Boston: Houghton Mifflin Co., 1925.

BALDWIN, CLARE C. *Organization and Administration of Substitute Teaching Service in City School Systems.* New York: Bureau of Publications, Teachers College, Columbia University, 1934.

BALLOU, FRANK W. *The Appointment of Teachers in Cities.* Cambridge, Mass.: Harvard University Press, 1915.

BENSON, W. W. "The Selection of Teachers." *Alabama School Journal*, 46: February, 1929.

BROGAN, WHIT. *The Work of Placement Offices in Teacher-Training Institutions.* New York: Bureau of Publications, Teachers College, Columbia University, 1930.

BUCKINGHAM, B. R. *Supply and Demand in Teacher Training.* Bureau of Educational Research Monograph No. 4. Columbus: Ohio State University, 1926.

CHARTERS, W. W. AND WAPLES, D., Directors. *The Commonwealth Teacher-Training Study.* Chicago: The University of Chicago Press, 1929.

COOKE, DENNIS H. *Problems of the Teaching Personnel.* New York: Longmans, Green and Co., 1933.

COOPER, HERMAN. "Report on Admission Regulations." *New York State Education*, December, 1935.

CUBBERLEY, ELLWOOD P. *The Portland Survey.* Yonkers-on-Hudson, N. Y.: The World Book Co., 1915.

————, *Public School Administration.* Boston: Houghton Mifflin Co., 1929.

DAVIS, CALVIN O. "What Qualifications Are Demanded of Teachers?" *Nation's Schools*, 3: January, February, May, and June, 1929.

DOUGLASS, HARL H. *Organization and Administration of Secondary Schools.* Boston: Ginn and Co., 1932.

DRAPER, A. S. *American Education.* Syracuse, N.Y.: Bardeen, Inc., 1909.

Education Law, State of New York. Albany: University of the State of New York Bulletin, 1936.

ELSBREE, WILLARD S. *Teachers' Salaries.* New York: Bureau of Publications, Teachers College, Columbia University, 1931.

ENGELHARDT, FRED. *Public School Organization and Administration.* Boston: Ginn and Co., 1931.

EVENDEN, E. S. "The Superintendent of Schools and the Education of Teachers." *Official Report*, Department of Superintendence of the National Education Association, Atlantic City Meeting. Washington, D.C.: National Education Association, 1935.

FALLS, J. D. "The Selection of Teachers for Classroom Instruction." *American School Board Journal*, November, 1932.

FOSTER, HERBERT H. *High School Administration*. New York: The Century Co., 1928.

FRANKLIN, RAY. "What Superintendents Ask Applying Teachers." *American School Board Journal*, April, 1930.

GRAVES, FRANK P. *The Administration of American Education*. New York: The Macmillan Co., 1932.

————, Director. *Report of a Survey of the Public Schools of New Rochelle*. New Rochelle, N.Y.: Board of Education, 1936.

JACOBSON, E. W. "How to Get Good Teachers." *School Management*, March, 1932.

KELLER, FRANK. "Use of Teachers' Application Blanks." University of Pittsburgh, Master's Thesis, 1928 (unpublished).

LEWIS, E. E. *Personnel Problems of the Teaching Staff*. New York: The Century Co., 1925.

MADSEN, I. N. "The Predicting of Teaching Success." *Educational Administration and Supervision*, January, 1927.

MAXWELL, C. R. AND KILZER, L. R. *High School Administration*. Garden City, N.Y.: Doubleday, Doran Co., Inc., 1936.

MORGAN, M. EVANS AND CLINE, ERVIN C. *Systematizing the Work of School Principals*. New York: Professional and Technical Press, 1930.

NATIONAL EDUCATION ASSOCIATION. Committee on Ethics of the Profession. *Ethics of the Teaching Profession*, Section 5, Article II, Philadelphia, 1926.

————, Department of Superintendence. *Twelfth Yearbook, Critical Problems in School Administration*. Washington, D.C., 1934.

————, Department of Superintendence. *Fifteenth Yearbook, The Improvement of Education*. Washington, D.C., 1937.

————, Department of Superintendence. *Official Report*, St. Louis Meeting. Washington, D.C.: National Education Association, 1936.

————, Research Division. "Practices Affecting Teacher Personnel." *Research Bulletin*, Vol. VI, No. 4, September, 1928.

————, Research Division. "Administrative Practices Affecting Classroom Teachers," Part I: The Selection and Appointment of Teachers. *Research Bulletin*, Vol. X, No. 1, January, 1932.

NATIONAL SURVEY OF THE EDUCATION OF TEACHERS. Volume II: *Teacher Personnel in the United States*. Washington, D.C.: U. S. Office of Education, 1933.

————. Volume III: *Teacher Education Curricula*. Washington, D.C.: U. S. Office of Education, 1933.

————. Volume VI: *Summary and Interpretations*. Washington, D.C.: U. S. Office of Education, 1933.

NEWLON, JESSE H. *Educational Administration as Social Policy*. Part III: Report of the Commission on the Social Studies, American Historical Association. New York: Charles Scribner's Sons, 1934.

NIETZ, JOHN A. "The Current Use of Teachers' Application Blanks." *American School Board Journal*, March, 1928.

POTTER, MILTON C. *Official Report*, Department of Superintendence of the National Education Association, Atlantic City Meeting. Washington, D.C.: National Education Association, 1935.

REEDER, WARD G. *The Fundamentals of Public School Administration.* New York: The Macmillan Co., 1930.

ROBINSON, WILLIAM McK. "Shall Untrained Persons Be Employed to Teach Our Children?" *School Life*, November, 1925.

RUGG, H. O. "Is the Rating of Human Character Practicable?" *Journal of Educational Psychology*, 13: 1922.

Rules and Regulations of City School Systems.

STEINER, M. A. "The Technic of Interviewing Teachers." *American School Board Journal*, June, 1928.

STRAYER, GEORGE D., Director. *Official Report of the Educational Survey Commission, State of Florida.* Senate and House of Representatives, Florida State Legislature, 1929.

————. *Report of the Survey of the Schools of Fort Worth, Texas.* New York: Bureau of Publications, Teachers College, Columbia University, 1931.

————. *Report of the Survey of the Schools of Chicago, Illinois.* Volume I. New York: Bureau of Publications, Teachers College, Columbia University, 1932.

SUHRIE, AMBROSE L. "The Superintendent of Schools and the Education of Teachers." *Official Report*, Department of Superintendence of the National Education Association, Atlantic City Meeting. Washington, D.C.: National Education Association, 1935.

SUZZALLO, HENRY. "Schools of a People." *Twenty-Sixth Annual Report of the President and of the Treasurer of the Carnegie Foundation for the Advancement of Teaching.* New York: The Carnegie Foundation, 522 Fifth Avenue, 1931.

SYMONDS, PERCIVAL M. *Diagnosing Personality and Conduct.* New York: The Century Co., 1931.

TIEGS, ERNEST W. *An Evaluation of Some Techniques of Teacher Selection.* Bloomington, Ill.: Public School Publishing Co., 1928.

————. *Tests and Measurements for Teachers.* Boston: Houghton Mifflin Co., 1931.

TUBBS, ESTON B. "The Selection of Teachers." *Peabody Journal of Education*, March, 1930.

WHITNEY, FREDERICK L. *The Growth of Teachers in Service.* New York: The Century Co., 1927.

VITA

JOHN COULBOURN was born August 26, 1888, in Somerset County, Maryland. He attended the public schools of Baltimore, graduating from the Baltimore City College in 1906 and from the Teachers Training School of Baltimore in 1907. He received the LL.B. degree from the University of Maryland in 1910; the B.S. degree from Johns Hopkins University in 1924; and the M.A. degree from Teachers College, Columbia University, in 1931. He was Assistant Critic Teacher at the Teachers Training School of Baltimore, 1907–1908; Vice-Principal, Public School No. 64, Baltimore, 1908–10; English Master, Tome School for Boys, Port Deposit, Maryland, 1910–1919; English Instructor, Baltimore City College, 1919–1923; Principal, Clifton Park Junior High School, Baltimore, 1923–1925; Assistant Superintendent, Secondary Education, Baltimore, 1925–1930; Principal, Junior and Senior High Schools, Garden City, Long Island, New York, 1931– ——.